Take a Walk
on the

Inside

EXPAND YOUR EMOTIONAL INTELLIGENCE

BUILD THE FOUNDATION FOR MASTERFUL LEADERSHIP

Take a Walk
on the

Inside

EXPAND YOUR EMOTIONAL INTELLIGENCE

TRUDY ANN PELLETIER

Take a Walk on the Inside

Build the Foundation for Masterful Leadership

Expand Your Emotional Intelligence

© 2016 by Trudy Ann Pelletier

Ebook ISBN: 978-0-9952296-1-7
Paperback ISBN: 978-0-9952296-0-0

Additional copies of this book may be ordered by visiting the PPG Online Bookstore at:

shop.polishedpublishinggroup.com

Due to the dynamic nature of the Internet, any website addresses mentioned within this book might have been changed or discontinued since its publication.

Table of Contents

My First Walk on the Inside

I'm standing in front of eight women while I'm being introduced by Joanne. I hardly know Joanne, having only recently met her for business reasons. She calls me with an invitation shortly after we met. I say "I'm busy, please call again." She calls every month for almost a year, with the same invitation: to attend an introduction to a "woman's workshop." Each time she invites me, I am busy. I wonder why a woman I hardly know is so tenacious and committed to me learning about this workshop. I am genuinely busy—doing, doing, doing. I'm not present to being driven by my need to prove I'm worthy, to show everyone I am a good human being, and to prove I matter and that I am lovable. I am unaware of my internal conversations about "not being enough" and "never being enough," regardless of how much I do. I am oblivious to the experience of compensating for the emptiness and ugliness I see and feel on the inside. I don't see that I'm working so hard to fill myself up from the outside in.

There I am in front of this group of ladies, and Joanne says, "This is Trudy. Don't let her fool you. She looks like she has it all together. Every hair is in place, she is dressed for success, and she looks perfect with matching shoes, purse and accessories. Everything about her looks good—and she is dying on the inside!"

I am stunned she knows. I am hardly willing or able to acknowledge the disparity between how I show up and look in my outer life and the misery and hopelessness I am living in my inner life. I don't want them to know. I don't want anyone to know. There is terror coursing through my body—and at the same time relief. I am exhausted from all the doing and all the pretending. I am so glad to be known and so afraid to be judged. Now that someone knows, perhaps I can stop pretending, perhaps I can rest. Perhaps I can stop trying to save the world, when really, it's me I'm trying to save; only I didn't know it then.

This is the beginning of "My Walk on the Inside."

I don't know where it will lead. I am scared of what I'll learn about myself;

afraid that what I will discover will validate "I'm not enough." I take the risk. I keep walking on the inside, recognizing with certainty that how I am living is not working.

As I look back, I realize I was living at the effect of life when I made the choice to "Take a Walk on the Inside." What I didn't know at the time is how much I was ruled by my past. I continue to discover where I am at the effect of life and circumstances; whether present day or from my past; something is running me.

When this happens, I "Take a Walk on the Inside" to meet myself.

"The unexamined life is not worth living."

~ Socrates (n.d.)

Acknowledgements

My Kids: Robbie and Alicia

I am blessed with and by you as the greatest gifts in my life. You are remarkable human beings. I am proud of who you are you today and who you are becoming, moment-by-moment. I love you.

My Big Sister: Diane

You are amazing—you are a blessing to me. You have been a lifeline for me. Thank you. With love.

My Family: Mom, Dad, Murray, Lela, Denis, Tom, Jordan, Karlee, Sebastien, Maurice, Marlene

I am grateful for you and all of the life experiences we have shared—every experience—a mixture of great moments and not-so-great moments. I see the perfection for me in all of our life shared. The contribution you and our experiences have made to me, in who I show up as in the world, and what I do. I am truly grateful for all of my life's experiences. I am at peace with what happened and didn't happen, with how life went and didn't go; and with who I thought I was and wasn't. With gratitude and love.

My Love: Tim Cousins

Meeting you awakened a deep knowing within me that you and I have great gifts for each other and to share with each other. Within a couple of days of meeting you, I found a wall plaque quoted by the great Gonzo, "There's not a word yet for OLD FRIENDS who've just met."

Thank you for being a "yes" to my possibility of creating exquisite love and partnership that lasts a lifetime. Thank you for choosing me. Thank you for your note after we met in person for the first time on May 18, 2015: "Time truly did stand still today…. With you, I would like to pursue the three elements we briefly touched upon. To give love, receive love, and pursue happiness." I love you, darling Tim.

An Angel: Ann Burgess

You altered my world when you started working with me in 2013. Thank you for being a friend, partner, colleague, and guardian for me.

My Friend and Book Coach: Don Greaves

I appreciate and value your friendship and commitment to me and to the planet. I remember the impact on me when you shared your story "Not on My Watch." Your heart, passion, and conviction touched me. This journey has been graced with all of that coupled with your guidance, love, and listening. With heartfelt gratitude for who you are—generous and caring contribution to the world. Thank you for having my back.

MY COMMITTED LISTENERS

Kevin Brown, Joy McTavish, Karen Dumontier, Allison McDougall, and Teresa Sulkin

You are special people whom I appreciate and value sharing my "Walks on the Inside." I would not be living a life I love, if it were not for your coaching and listening for my potential fulfilled—my greatness. You are and you make a difference. With love and appreciation.

MY COMMUNITY

I am blessed and grateful for an abundance of supporters, friends, family and colleagues. Not everyone is named; and if you aren't named, I trust you know who you are to me and for me.

Dana Morkeburg, Henry Kutarna, Judith Ravensbergen, Don Zinyk, Shauna Feth, Suze Casey, Adam Joyce, Todd Coleman, Ruth Steverlynck, Brian Lanier, Cindy Marks, Lionel Dumontier, Rael Kalley, Shannon Leigh, Greg Helfrich, Sharon Olynyck, Mike Mahannah, Laura Watson, Janice Kobelsky, Dick Frenz, Joanne Lawson, Pat Pitsel, Peter Naaykens, John and Faye Fisher.

INFLUENCERS

I am grateful to those teachers, authors and leaders who courageously confronted themselves in order to create and share their work with the world.

Some of my favourites are:

Conversations with God (Neale Donald Walsch), *The Power of Personal Accountability* (Mark Samuel and Sophie Chiche), *Fierce Conversations* (Susan Scott), *Landmark Worldwide* (Werner Erhard and Company), *The Art of Possibility* (Benjamin and Rosamund Stone Zander), *How to Win Friends and Influence People* (Dale Carnegie), *The Fifth Discipline* (Peter Senge), *Five Dysfunctions of a Team* (Patrick Lencioni), *Loving What Is* (Byron Katie), *The Gifts of Imperfection* (Brene Brown), *Belief Repatterning* (Suze Casey), *The Astonishing Power of Emotions: Let Your Feelings be Your Guide* (Esther and Jerry Hicks (the Teachings of Abraham)), and the series of work by Catherine Ponder.

YOU

It is with heartfelt gratitude and appreciation that I acknowledge you; those of you I know intimately and those I know only in sharing the experience of being human. Thank you for allowing me to join you for a few steps on your journey. I am grateful for the opportunity to be contribution. I consider it an extraordinary privilege that you have invited me to share myself with you. Thank you for being willing to let yourself see yourself in the stories and for being willing to explore.

Who you are for me is a miracle who has the power to become anyone you desire to be. I don't know your personal story, circumstances or private desires and dreams. I do know you as a human being. As human beings, we are much more alike than we are different. As human beings we tend to be far more familiar with our shortcomings than our strengths. I know your greatness!

You are courageous.

You are curiously engaged on a journey.

You are yearning for "more."

You are playing big; living a large life.

You have an appetite to discover something…
	You may not know what it is…You sense it's big!

PROMISE

MY PROMISE TO YOU

I promise you opportunities for discovery—many of them.

WHO I AM FOR YOU

I am someone who walks this journey, a fellow traveller; only, I've discovered there's no place to get to.

I am someone who believes in you, and the spirit and potential in humanity. I believe in miracles and possibilities. I believe in the personal power within you, and in every human being, to create and live an extraordinary and fulfilling life.

I am a stand for you.

I am a stand for humanity.

INVITATION

My invitation to you is for you to "Take a Walk on the Inside." Enjoy your journey of discovery.

With Love and Appreciation,

Connected Always
Trudy

FAMILY — OUR FOUNDATION

The root of your old ways of doing things goes back to your family experiences from childhood and adolescence. If you backtrack through the development of a problem, you will come to the root of it in your early family life. You can move far from the places where you were born and raised, and you can cut yourself off completely from all family members. However, your attitudes and behaviour are still primarily shaped by your family experiences from the past. These experiences created your psychological root system.

"Family patterns are so powerful partly because they grow out of instinctual need. The influence of family patterns is subtle and complex, touching all areas of your life in deep and often hidden ways." (Foster, 1993, pp. 22–23, 27)

That being said, there are four options:

Be exactly like your mother.

Be exactly like your father.

Not be exactly like your mother.

Not be exactly like your father.

I say again, I am at peace with every experience from my past. I am complete with my parents. I am grateful for every experience. As I continue to discover the "unknown, already existing" from my past, I believe I have everything I need to create and live an extraordinary life I love.

Mom, Dad, and Maurice

My siblings: Diane, Murray, and Lela

Thank you

With Love

What people say about Trudy

I have known Trudy for many years in both a personal and professional relationship. I have both trained Trudy and been trained by her. I have coached Trudy and have been coached by her. We spend many hours exchanging viewpoints and discussing the human condition. I acknowledge Trudy for the greatest compliment I can give.

Trudy lives an examined life. What does that mean? Trudy—through introspection, conversation and reading—is on the journey to discover what it means to be a human being both for herself, and more importantly, what she can share with others from her own examined experiences. Examined as an internal journey, a journey of self-discovery.

This book is a testament to her journey and her ability to make a difference with her words.

Don Greaves, P.Eng.
IBM Canada

Trudy is a passionate and creative family business facilitator in the family business space who authentically cares about her clients. I grew up in a family business, and today I lead it as we head into the fourth generation. What Trudy brings to the table to help solve issues and move the business and its leaders forward is the right stuff. She operates at that point where the family dynamic and the business imperative intertwine. I've seen her in action—she is a breath of fresh air in a field that used to be owned by the big consulting firms. They don't get family business. Trudy does.

Henry Kutarna, B.A. Hons. (Econ.), C.D.M.E., CMC, CEO
Kutarna Capital Corporation

I am at my first conference for professional speakers, where I bump into Trudy as we simultaneously pull out our chairs at back-to-back tables. We say hello, and engage in conversation to meet each other. I am struck by Trudy's ability to listen and connect with me as though she has known me for years. While one might expect someone to act like they're listening—especially during a professional conference—this was no "act." Trudy connects with people.

I've had the pleasure of participating in literally dozens of seminar sessions with Trudy over many years. She engages with a commitment to discovering who people truly are; and in the process discovers who she herself gets to be in each conversation.

If you're up for a journey through the peaks and valleys of life, Trudy is the perfect Sherpa.

Brian Lanier, President
The Leaders Circle

I love Trudy. She is that beautiful woman who walks into a room and completely owns it. Trudy knows who she is and what she's up to. She is the most interesting mix of power and humanity and she gives you complete freedom to be that too. Trudy is always striving to be her best self, and her enthusiasm for life is completely contagious.

J. MacTavish
Field Sales Associate

Every person has a purpose. As evidenced by the following pages, few people embrace their purpose with the passion and generosity that Trudy brings to all she does.

Trudy has a gift for communicating difficult issues with warmth, sensitivity, and compassion. This book is no exception.

D. A. Zinyk, FCPA, ICD
Consultant to Business Families

I limp stiffly to the bathroom, my knees, ankles, shoulders in pain, my inflammatory arthritis flaring! I limp back into the room, and sit on the bed in our hotel room, avoiding Trudy's eye knowing I have pushed my body past what it can tolerate.

"What goes on for you that you don't tell me how you really are when I check in?" Trudy asks.

I am silent, wanting to disappear into the bed covers. Trudy waits. "I didn't want to slow you down; I thought I would be okay today," I say, with a tremor in my voice. More silence.

"What else?' she asks.

With tears rolling down my cheeks, I sputter, "I didn't want to appear weak!"

"Do you get that telling me how it is for you allows me to contribute to you; and that is what makes you powerful?" Trudy says.

And like the truck that has hit me physically, I see my need to be tough, stubborn, independent, on my own for what it is; a story that constrains me and others. Today I am free to allow others to contribute to me without it meaning I am weak. I am free to ask for and accept help, support and care.

Karen

Trudy has helped me and ELRUS successfully navigate a number of difficult and complex high-stakes situations where failure would result in ruined careers, relationships, and failed business initiatives. Her courage, consciousness, and knowledge have made a remarkable difference in my career and personal life.

Greg Helfrich, National Operations Manager
ELRUS Aggregate Systems

As we explore the circumstances together, Trudy discovers for herself the pattern that is present. "Oh my God, I have an unfulfilled expectation," she declares.

"You do, don't you," I respond. She shares that she was being vulnerable in making a request; something she as a powerful, can-do person has rarely done.

"Here I am opening myself up and he doesn't even hear my request," she says, laughing out loud!

The Trudy I know is a powerful, energetic, and accomplished woman who at times forgets the gift she is to all who know her. In our conversation I remind her that we each are indeed a GIFT to the planet, exactly the way we are and the way we are not.

Our challenge is to remember who we are and to be grounded in a deep appreciation of our gifts. Looking back on this conversation, I can see the power of starting each day by declaring who we are for the planet.

Imagine a declaration that states "Who I am is *accomplished, vulnerable, playful, and prepared for action*." What might that enable?

Kevin Brown, ACC, I.S.P., ITCP, FCI
Chair, 641

Definitions

At the effect of life… When I say "at the effect of life," I am describing an experience of not having choice or having a say in how you show up in the face of condition(s) or circumstance(s). It's the experience of not being in command or control of one's thoughts and feelings and, therefore, actions. It is the feeling of being a victim and at the impact of life circumstances or others.

Distinguish… When I say "distinguish," I am implying that a particular thought, belief, conclusion, or discovery is noteworthy. There is value in distinguishing that particular thought, belief, conclusion, or discovery given it most likely is foundational to who we believe ourselves to be or what we believe is possible for our life.

Occur/Occurs… When I say "occur or occurs," I am speaking to a unique occurrence (experience) of an event that is created by one's context (how one thinks about and views an event). The same event occurs differently for each human being.

Cause… When I say "cause," I mean the "one" who owns the responsibility to produce, or generate, a specific result.

Contribution… means being someone who is and makes a positive difference to and for others in any number of ways.

Have the experience of being… When I say "have the experience," I am distinguishing that life is a series of events and our experience is created by our filters (thoughts, emotions or feelings, and attitudes), yet many of us live as though we are our thoughts, emotions, feelings and attitudes.

Be / Being… When I say "be or being," I am referencing the energy state one is in each moment. Our ways of being are a source of the actions we take or don't take and how we say what we say, including the words we choose. Our ways of being have impact on others, ourselves, and our experience of life itself.

1. The Framework

WHAT THIS BOOK IS ABOUT

THIS BOOK IS ABOUT DISCOVERY

I'm standing at the top of the stairs at eight years old, watching my mom and my step-dad beat my nine-year-old sister Diane. I am screaming for them to stop with tears streaming down my face. They don't. Right there, I make several decisions about me, about family, about love, about life. This event triggers a whole world of impact—only I have no memory of the decisions I, as an eight-year-old, make. This is what becomes my "unknown" already existing.

> *"The real voyage of discovery consists not in seeking new landscapes, but in having new eyes."*
>
> ~ Marcel Proust (n.d.)

Discovering what?

That which is "unknown or unseen." There are two kinds of "unknown or unseen," in essence, two sides of the same coin. One side of the coin is the unknown or unseen that already exists: decisions made, beliefs lived out—all impacts from our past. This already existing, yet unknown background is the lens through which we live and experience life.

The "unknown and unseen" on the other side of the coin is potential, creation; possibility. It is the pure creative life-force energy available to every human being, enabling each of us to create an extraordinary and fulfilling life founded on unlimited possibilities and miracles.

Right now, notice what you are thinking. Notice what you are saying to yourself about the words you just read. Notice what you are saying to yourself about what is possible for you, and what's not possible. Observe the shaping of what you do and don't do next is directly correlated to your thinking. Said another way, this is the lens through which you see and experience yourself and your life.

In this moment, you can "Take a Walk on the Inside" to see what is not known by you that has you intrigued or turned-off as you close the book. There is no wrong choice and there is no right choice. There is only choice coupled with the opportunity to be curious about the "unknown" that has you choose to do what you do. We talk ourselves "in" and "out" of doing "this" or "that" every time we take action. Being curious about the internal conversation that has you do "this" or do "that" is a key element of taking a walk on the inside.

The human being who decides not to continue to read, typically, will put their attention on the book subject matter. It is common to point to something outside of ourselves (blame/make wrong) versus confronting our own views, thinking, and beliefs that have us possibly making the same choices. You will have your reasons for choosing to close the book, which may sound like, "it doesn't resonate with me, or it doesn't make sense to me, or it's bull crap or it's weird, etc." Notice your internal conversation behind your decision.

Will you continue to read? Are you confronted by the words and ideas on the page? Does your belief system have you lean in to the opportunity to learn more about yourself through the book, or does it have you close the book, already deciding it's not for you? It's our thinking that shapes and moulds the life-force energy into our circumstances, conditions, limitations, and experiences.

What are you discovering about your internal conversation within the background of your choices and actions?

THIS BOOK IS ABOUT WONDER

> *"The world is full of magic things, patiently waiting for our senses to grow sharper."*
>
> ~ W.B. Yeats (n.d.)

Don says to me, "You don't know yourself without your drive. You don't know life without being driven."

I look at him like he has three heads. "No," I say with a low-grade anxiety growing into fear.

He says, "What if you lived your life already being accomplished? What if you could relax and be at ease doing what you are doing?"

Again, I look at him like he has three heads, as he is describing a life foreign to me. I take in his words and I relax myself, allowing my imagination to connect with his questions and ideas. I discover I have not ever considered living life from a place of already being accomplished, already being successful, already being worthy. I begin to wonder what my life and what my experience of myself and my relationships could be if I lived from the place of being accomplished, successful, worthy and valuable. I discover a new possibility: a life of ease, joy, and freedom.

> *"Wonder is the beginning of wisdom."*
>
> *~ Socrates (n.d.)*

Wonder what?

Wonder about anything and everything; wherever your heart's desires and limitless imagination takes you. I am not talking about wishing and wanting. Wonder is different. We all have wants, wishes, and in some instances, needs for our life to be different than what it is. Wishing, wanting, needing more money, more time, more love, more happiness; or wishing, wanting, needing less stress, less weight, less pressure, less or more of "something." None of that is wonder.

It takes a certain mindset or head and heart space to "wonder." It takes a clear mind, a space on the inside allowing our mind to explore, to imagine and to discover. Being in "wonder" is where we as kids lived and played a lot of our time. However, as we grow into adults, we lose this sense of "wonder." Wonder is an uncommon and unique experience to us as adults. We lose the childlike play of wondering and imagination in the process of growing older.

As a verb, "wonder" means to think or speculate curiously, to be filled with admiration, amazement or awe; marvel. As a noun, the definition of "wonder" is something strange and surprising; a cause of surprise, astonishment or admiration, miraculous deed or event; remarkable phenomenon; the emotion excited by what is strange and surprising, a feeling of surprised or puzzled interest, sometimes tinged with admiration. (www.dictionary.com, 2016).

You could wonder about how fulfilling and nourishing your relationships could be. You could wonder about what it's like to be free and to be happy. You could wonder about what it would be like to love your husband or wife again, like you did when you first fell in love with that marvelous human being. You could wonder about how it would be if you owned your magnificence. You could wonder about being alive and vital in your life exactly as it is and exactly as it isn't.

"In my travels I found no answers, only wonders."

~ Marty Rubin (n.d.)

What is your experience of yourself as you let yourself wonder?

THIS BOOK IS ABOUT QUESTIONS

— BIG QUESTIONS THAT CAUSE A PAUSE;

AND THEN…

DISCOVERY

*"The important thing is not to stop questioning.
Curiosity has its own reason for existing."*

~ Albert Einstein (n.d.)

There are opportunities I call gifts, in both asking and answering questions. Real questions that uncover what really matters to you, and others and what you or they are really dealing with. Revealing questions that give you access to discovering your blind spots and the magnificent beauty within. Connecting questions that cause new thinking, shifts in paradigms, and whole-hearted responses. Courageous questions that generate risk and an invitation that creates the experience of being heard, seen, and understood. Profound questions that lead you to wonder, love, and forgiveness. Vulnerable questions that yield compassion, surrender, acceptance, and responsibility; all inter-mingled resulting in authentic personal power.

I am facilitating round two of a strategic planning session with nine executives, approximately three weeks after the first round. We're an hour or so into the conversation, and I know there is an elephant in the room. I don't know what it is; I do know there is something in the space. As I listen to their conversation, a few of the executives occur to me as three-year-old boys having a tantrum. There is upset in the background and a high degree of mistrust in the room.

I say, "Gentlemen, I don't know what is going on. I do know that we aren't going to get any meaningful planning done if we don't deal with what is going on in the background." They look at me—silence. I wait. One of them poses a question to those in the room. It's a question that doesn't land in a way that gives access to anything new. Actually it's a superficial question and appears incongruent with the heaviness in the room. I ask, "Daryl, what is the real question behind your question?" He is startled, the silence is deafening, the suspension is engrossing, and the vulnerability is palpable.

He slowly turns to the president and says, "Are you planning to leave the company?" As the president starts to respond, the space in the room opens up and people once again are breathing. As the team engages with more questions, the conversation eventually frees them up to be present and work on the strategy as intended.

What is the question you have of yourself that you've been unwilling to ask of yourself?

Questions don't come naturally to us. As human beings, we like to know, we like to have the answers; and in many instances we believe we need to know. We are trained to know at an early age, given the pats and rewards when we raise our hand in school and have the right answer. We grow up developing our bank of what we know; and go into the majority of our conversations with the intention to convince people to adopt our way of thinking or defending what we know. It is rare to be in an agenda-free conversation; one that is opinion and answer free where the only goal is to be with and understand the other person. Conversations where we find ourselves being in a state of wonder and curiously engaged with the other person are rare. This means we are naturally asking questions (and more questions, and then more questions) in order to truly appreciate and understand the person and/or issue in front of us.

"Staying in the question means being okay with the ambiguous. Being okay with ambiguity means being open to the possible...Live in your question until you can see the vast panorama of possible answers." (Hurson, 2008, pp. 56, 65)

If you could be anybody, would you be yourself?

THIS BOOK IS ABOUT APPETITE

I have an insatiable appetite for learning. Learning, for me, is fuel. Learning something new pulls me forward; it pulls me through and out of the breakdowns in life. Learning urges me to keep going and to never give up. To what end, you might ask. To be bigger, better, and to live life larger. Learning drives progress, expansion, growth and newness.

The kind of learner I am now is quite different than when I was younger and less aware of my background internal conversations. As a learner today, I am newly curious in that I make myself park what it is I think I know, or know that I know. I curiously stand in the idea and space of knowing nothing, thereby creating room to truly learn.

> *"Empty your cup so that it may be filled; become devoid to gain totality."*
>
> ~ *Bruce Lee (n.d.)*

What kind of learner are you?

Notice what you are saying to yourself about who you are as a learner and the kind of learner you are. As you pay attention to what you are saying about yourself to yourself, notice the judgments you may have about what you see. In the work I do, I often hear people describe themselves as open-minded learners. I then observe that when they are presented with an idea that doesn't align with their beliefs and experiences, they throw away the idea, justifying and rationalizing doing so.

Imagine that everything learned becomes a wall of bricks; each of us has a personal wall of bricks representing all learning. When we are learning, one of two things happens: If what we have learned fits in with our walls of bricks, it gets added to the wall of bricks. If what we have learned doesn't fit in with our walls of bricks, the learning is discarded and justifications and rationalizations are given for why it is invalid. True learning is accepting new things and letting our walls of bricks be disassembled by new ideas.

> People who "know" can tell you all the things that can't be done and why. People who "know" don't need to learn because they already have the answers. People who "know" are complete—or perhaps just finished. More often than not, people who "know" are also people who "no." But knowingness is not the same as knowledge. Knowingness is sealed; nothing can get in. Knowledge is open. Knowingness sees challenge as a threat. Knowledge sees challenge as opportunity. Knowingness is a portcullis that helps us feel secure. Knowledge is a road to new horizons. (Hurson, 2008, p. 56)

> *"Man cannot discover new oceans unless he has the courage to lose sight of the shore."*
>
> *~ André Gide (n.d.)*

What will you park—put aside—to be learning newly as you move through the pages?

My coach shares his commitment to live an "upset free" life. He has my attention! I have not thought of or imagined an upset free life as a possible way to live life—ever. It's not in my paradigm—it's such a foreign thought that initially I struggle to imagine it. What would life be like without upset? I wonder who I could be so that I have an upset free life. I wonder who I would need to be to create an upset free life. I wonder how extraordinary my experience of myself and others would be. Again, I struggle to remain in the possibility of living an upset free life. As I do so, I realize I have a growing appetite for what is unknown to me. As I consider living an upset free life, I realize I have no idea what will be required of me to create that kind of life. As I play with this in my mind, I am present to choice. I can take on the game of choosing to live an upset free life, imagining the adventure, the discovery, and the possibilities of knowing, and being bigger than I know myself to be.

You might be wondering if I am winning at the game of an "upset free" life. Yes! Absolutely. I live upset free in more moments than if I had not been playing to live life upset free. Through the game, I am expanding my capacity to be upset free. This gives me opportunities to discover my greatness in moments. I am living the possibility of living an upset free life, creating from a space of nothing—pure potential—enjoying peace, trust, and light-heartedness.

As human beings, we have a natural yearning for "more." Regardless of where we are in life, successful and accomplished or struggling and stressed, there is a desire for something more. Our life-force energy is urging newness, craving expansion, aspiring; as nature itself is progressive, is designed to grow, advancing evolution. Regardless of conditions and circumstances, nature is meant to grow. And so it does! When I'm out hiking, I love being present to the miracles in and of nature: a spruce tree growing in what seems to be impossible conditions and circumstances given the terrain of rock. This is true for each of us as human beings. Something in each of us is designed to grow, to expand, to desire more. Naturally so—regardless of circumstance or condition!

As we have a higher aspiration or vision for ourselves, we may see ourselves as someone who cannot yet fulfill that vision. If all we do is say "yes" to that vision while holding it firmly in our mind, we are on the journey to "become" the person who can deliver on that vision. We have the power to become "anyone and anything," and this becoming is infinite. As we are fulfilling that vision and being that "bigger / best" person, a higher aspiration for something more emerges. Again, we may not yet be the person who can deliver that vision; and again, as we say "yes" to the vision, we become the person who is expanded in some way.

Growth is inherent in human nature.

I laugh at myself for the audacity I had in thinking I could stop nature. Four years ago, I hire a landscaper. His task is to lay a new stone sidewalk in my backyard, and to replace the small patch of weeds between my house and my neighbour's with gravel. I say to him, "Look at the grass and the weeds coming up in the cracks. I want you to make sure nothing will grow. I don't want to deal with pulling weeds and grass between the stones."

He says, "No problem, I'll lay three layers of landscape fabric." I believe him.

Today, that patch of gravel is fraught with grass and weeds, quite tall because it isn't a terrain I can use my lawnmower on. My beautiful stone sidewalk has become green; both weeds and grass are popping up between the stones in the cracks that were once filled with sand. I actually thought I could stop nature from growing. I have one of two choices: I can either laugh at myself or be critical of myself for thinking I could stop nature—and then, of course, spending all that money on it. There was a time when I would have been the critic; now I'm choosing the alternative. The bigger lesson for me is remembering that the forces of nature are within me and each one of us. Choosing to align with the forces of nature enable me to create a life I love.

What do you want more of?

Who are you aspiring to become?

What do you have an appetite for?

WHAT THIS BOOK IS NOT ABOUT

ANSWERS — I DON'T HAVE YOUR ANSWERS

> *"At the center of your being, you have the answer;*
> *you know who you are and you know what you want."*
>
> ~ Lao Tzu (n.d.)

A 56-year-old man sits across from me behind his desk as he says, "It was so nice to meet you last week at the breakfast meeting."

"Thank you, and likewise," I say. While I don't know him, and I am unclear on his purpose for our meeting, I am deliberate in my presence and attentiveness. He looks at me expectantly. I smile and I wait, being generous. He looks at me and starts to cry. I sit with him, being open and available to the experience of his emotions and the conversation he has invited me to. He says nothing for several minutes, dealing with the tears rolling down his face uncontrollably, as I sit there silently offering patience and acceptance.

He says, "I knew you would be someone who is okay with tears when life is falling apart." More tears. I wait in unspoken serenity, sitting with his vulnerability and trust. He shares, "My wife is leaving me, my son doesn't connect with me, my business is off the rails—I am in trouble. I have nowhere to go. I don't know what to do."

"What else?" I ask. He answers, "My partners are abandoning the business; I will be devastated."

"How can I help?" I inquire.

He implores, "Tell me what to do!" I remain quiet as he contemplates his life, his challenges, worries and fears.

"I don't have your answers. No one has your answers." Silence. "I invite you to consider that your answers are not in what you know. Your answers are a discovery; you are the only one who can discover them." I suggest.

He looks at me. He's thoughtful and then says, "I get that."

"It takes immense courage to be willing to meet ourself in Silence."

~ Christina Feldman (2003)

I laugh at myself as I reflect on the numerous times I thought I had answers. My mind was made up—I was sure I knew how it was for me and how life was going to go. Surprise! Life goes a completely different way, often to my delight, and in a way I had not considered. Miracles! In these moments, I remember I do not have the answers; and I am present to the value of coming from knowing nothing.

Other occasions and more often than I want to admit, I actually think I have the answers for others. I assume I know them, I understand what they're dealing with and how it is for them. I proceed to give answers, telling them who they could be, how they could be better, and how if they thought or acted a certain way, life for them would be great. This never goes well!

I liken it to building muscle; whereby, day after day, we deliberately pick up the weights, do the program to build our body. An underdeveloped muscle in most of us is setting aside what we know: the muscle of parking our own interests and perspectives, giving up the conclusions and answers we've already jumped to, so we can be curious in our conversations, asking questions, wondering and discovering—all nourished by a big appetite to learn and understand.

It's been a journey of discovery to step into knowing nothing; said another way, an empty space. Whether I am clearing myself to be in a coaching conversation with someone, to facilitate a meaningful dialogue or simply to be present and available for myself or another, I have built the muscle to be able to give up knowing, give up the need for answers, and give up needing certainty. This is part of the game of personal mastery.

"It seems clear that consciously or not, human beings will do almost anything to avoid the ambiguity of not knowing." (Hurson, 2008, p. 64)

If you let yourself be comfortable not knowing, what questions would you live in?

FIXES — THIS BOOK IS NOT ABOUT FIXING

We come at life, both challenges and people, like there is something to fix. This includes ourselves in that in the face of our belief that all human beings are flawed, we share in a mindset we need to be fixed.

> *"The greatest thing in the world is to know how to belong to oneself."*
>
> *~ Michel de Montaigne, The Complete Essays (Trans. by Screech, 1989.)*

I'm on stage, speaking to 1,400 people at a Dale Carnegie International Conference. "I'm with a young entrepreneur who shares all his dreams and passions for his business and his family." I say.

He tells me that he is afraid to speak in public, and he knows he will need that skill to fulfill on all his goals. He doesn't register for the Dale Carnegie course. His fear is bigger than his dream—his fear is bigger than he knows himself to be.

I pull out a personal cheque, and I sign it, saying "I will personally guarantee your success to overcome your fears of speaking in public." He looks at me as I pause. I persist with, "All you have to do is show up and participate. I'll give you this cheque to cash at the end of the program if you have not conquered your fear of public speaking." I am convinced he'll overcome his fear, and in doing so he will discover how big he is. I believe with my whole heart he can do this, and given that I am out to fix and save people from themselves, the Dale Carnegie course is the fix.

Looking back, I see I was only trying to fix and save me. I have since discovered there is nothing and no one to fix. Today, I deliberately seek to discover and see the perfection in everything, standing inside of "nothing is wrong and there is nothing to fix," moment-by-moment.

If my language is unfamiliar to you, it's an invitation to pay attention to the internal conversation inherent in being human. It shows up in how we speak about things, and the patterned way we live in the world. Human beings, you and I, have a default way of living which is the "either / or" world. We live most of our life taking a point of view, making a judgment in which we oscillate between opposite positions. Being "either right or wrong" and "either good or bad" are examples of common patterned views of the world. These judgments are programmed in our lenses; we rarely think about them, and therefore don't challenge them. Our judgment creates a reaction such that we come into situations and at people armed to convince, defend, fix, explain, tell, justify, and blame, to give some examples.

Today I choose to live life from the belief that we are all "perfectly imperfect" and there is nothing to fix.

The patriarch says, "I want you to fix them." It's a business family in crisis due to a conflict between siblings. "This can't go on any longer," he continues, "I need to know if I have to act on plan B. If they can't get their stuff fixed, I'll just sell the whole damn business!"

What is available to you when you stand in the idea that there is nothing and no one wrong, and nothing and no one to fix?

2. Discover What?

"You cannot teach a man anything. You can only help him discover it within himself."

~ *Galileo Galilei (n.d.)*

Discoveries are the outcomes of a certain mindset; that of an adventurer, traveller or seeker. A mindset is a combination of ways of being and acting such that the result is discovery.

Being curious is a powerful state as we are naturally (without will or effort) asking questions, exploring, leaning in, listening, reflecting, and engaging in people and experiences. Curiosity innately generates learning and understanding.

Being compassionate with oneself and others generates a space for discovery. I fell in love with the definition of being "compassionate" when I participated in Michael Brown's work called the Presence Process (2010). This definition has really served me on my journey and is, "I'm willing to see the other person is doing the best they can," and for myself, "I'm willing to see in this moment that I'm doing the best I can (even if I know better)." I don't have to be compassionate; being willing to be compassionate is enough to create a space for learning, reflection and discoveries. For many of us, what is right there is criticism, judgment, and making others or ourselves wrong, all of which trigger our brain into survival mode, which in turn blocks learning, thereby stopping discovery of anything new.

Being courageously committed is an empowering mindset that I assert is essential to Taking a Walk on the Inside.

"If it were easy, everyone would be doing it."

~ *Tom Hanks, A League of Their Own (1992)*

Who would you be if you were causing discoveries?

It is for you to answer that question.

My intention is to be contribution to you. Through my shares, the questions asked, the opportunity to reflect, and the invitation to Take a Walk on the Inside is that you discover your greatness and your personal power. It is my desire that you connect to your personal power, giving you access to fulfill the aspirations you have of and for yourself, and for your life.

What you will discover is not known to me. Enjoy your journey!

THE KNOWN AND THE NOT KNOWN

"I know one thing; that I know nothing."

~ Socrates (n.d.)

There are any number of dynamics playing out at any given moment, some of which are known and some of which are unknown. Even though I believe there are more "unknowns" than what I'm speaking to, I am demonstrating the power and impact of things known and not known. My share illustrates the multiple dynamics at play in any given situation. This is a common experience for us as human beings.

It's June 2009, and the end of my third year in business is around the corner. I'm not where I thought I would be in terms of success and making money; in fact, I'm not even close. I'm struggling to pick up the phone to get in front of people. I'm paralyzed with fear of not making it, I'm beating myself up for being so lost, and I'm worrying and wishing my life was different. I have no energy, little focus, and I have pressure as I am beyond the edge of my financial comfort zone. I have the experience of being powerless, frustrated, isolated, and unhappy.

*I **know** one of the things I do well and effortlessly is helping speakers to become better at presenting themselves and their ideas. I need an injection of cash and the solution is an email marketing campaign to promote "Core Skills for Dynamic Presentations." My website team and I design a world-class campaign, pick a date for release, and rent an email list of 8,000 Calgary business leaders. I pay the invoice and they press send.*

*Within two days, I have several thousand hits on my website—in fact, I have 4,573 hits—yet only two leads. I don't get it. I **know** there is a need for public speaking skills, and I **know** I am good at this. I panic as turmoil and fear grabs a stronger hold on both my head and my heart. I am out of money and I am out of time! I am stopped. I have the experience of falling apart, being on an emotional roller coaster of self-pity, tears, and fears. I am so angry at myself for not working harder, for taking the risks, for putting my house and savings on the line, and for even thinking I could be successful as a business owner. There is a world not known to me inside of my thinking playing out and I don't know it. I am living into a future of losing everything.*

*The **not known** gripping me is a decision I unconsciously made: the decision to take the results of this campaign as a sign whether or not I keep my business alive. I **unknowingly** rigged it that if this campaign isn't successful I will quit. I believe I will fail if I don't generate an injection of revenue. I'm done. I'll give up on my dreams and go get a job. I am face-to-face with failure, and I'm discovering the power of the **not known** decision. I am paralyzed and I don't know what to do or where to turn. I'm not thinking clearly in the face of being a failure. I feel sorry for myself; I feel guilty, ashamed, and embarrassed. I am at the effect of the results, actually the lack of results. I am at the effect of my experience and my feelings. I have the experience of no power, and I have no say in how my life is going to go.*

Six weeks later, I'm sitting with Ric Durrant over lunch. I am sharing with him what happened, and I'm crying. I still don't have it together. Ric says, "Forty-five hundred hits on your website, and only two leads. What message on your website is turning people off?" In that moment, I shift. I stop feeling sorry for myself, and I step into learning.

It is amazing how much I am learning about myself right now as I write this book. I'm discovering who I can be through the experience of writing this book. My discoveries have been a mix of a familiar view or experience and new encounters, some of which pop and pass quickly. Other discoveries occur as a sustaining experience lived longer.

I'm in Canmore, staying in a glorious condo for eight days to write. Every view I have is so beautiful; I'm discovering silence and its power. I am alive on the inside, newly present to nature and life-force energy. I'm discovering flow, as in streaming ideas and words; flow, as in ease in just making something; flow, as in movement and strength as I run along the river, purposefully rejuvenating myself. I'm discovering how to let myself receive support from others, as my friend (and now book coach) Don talks with me every day; all in support of fulfilling my goal. I'm discovering what it is to be free and accepting of the good, the bad, and the ugly of breakdowns while I write. I'm discovering how much I love language and how, at times, language falls short of what I want to share.

What an adventure!

> *"You can't un-ring a bell."*
> *~ David Foster Wallace (n.d.)*

You can't un-discover something you've discovered!

What ways of being and acting are you taking on to create discovery?

INHERENT TO HUMAN BEINGS

THE NEED TO BE RIGHT

Monkeys are baited and captured by using what is of value to them—their food. In the body of the trap is a banana, which is valuable to monkeys. The trap has a narrow entrance, designed so the monkey can put its arm in to pick up the banana; however, the monkey cannot remove its arm while hanging onto the banana. All the monkey would have to do is let go of the banana and it would be free. However, it doesn't let go; it wants the banana and the banana is in its hand. A person comes along, throws a sack over the monkey's head, and the moment it's in the dark, it lets go of the banana.

I liken this to human beings with our ideas and opinions. We hang onto them at all costs. We love our own opinions, views, and perspectives.

We hang onto them at the expense of our relationships, peace of mind, well-being, and happiness; just like the monkey hangs onto the banana at the expense of freedom.

"Would you rather be happy or be right?"

~ Unknown

Inherent to human beings is the need to be right. We argue for our opinions and perspectives at the expense of love and affinity. We are self-interested beings wired for self-preservation. Being right is a form of survival, often providing us with the experience of being in control. It's an automatic mechanism that arises out of fear of being wrong and a need to make sense of the world and fit it into our views, beliefs, and perspectives. Most of us grapple at the core with being inadequate, small, and not enough. Being right is a form of defending and protecting ourselves.

George is saying "I've been president of our family business for twelve years. I don't own any of it. My dad is 75 years old; he's not been working in the business for a long time now. He is unwilling to have any conversation about transferring ownership. Dad has said we can all deal with it after he is gone. This is frustrating. I am angry. I am dealing with three family members in the business in conflict with each other, and my hands are tied. I don't have any real authority. I am worried these three are going to be made my partners, and I won't have any say over it. I need my dad to transfer the ownership. How can you help us?" I ask a few more questions to understand the situation. As I clarify the history and present challenges, I offer a course of action to explore.

He says, "That won't work; Dad won't have the conversation." I ask more questions. I offer an alternative pathway to engaging the family in the conversation only to have George say, "That won't work; Dad won't have the conversation." This happens two more times. I invite George to consider that his certainty in knowing what his dad is going to say and what he is going to do in any of the four different options is the biggest barrier to moving this forward. I stop talking and wait. George says, "I know my Dad. I've tried everything."

I continue, "Notice how right you are being. You are right about having tried everything. You are right about what your dad is and isn't going to do. You are right about your hands being tied. You are right about how nothing will change. You are right about it all, so there is no possibility and therefore no room to take any action. Do you want to be happy or do you want to be right?

George looks perplexed. "But I know my dad, Trudy," as he continues to say more about what he knows.

I ask George a very simple question, "What is your dad afraid of?"

George says, "I don't know."

"You could give up what you believe and think you know about your dad. Are you interested in knowing what he is really dealing with?" George is seeing something new—he has access to a new world. George's dad becomes a human being dealing with something, rather than the thing George made him out to be: uncaring, stubborn, and untrusting. George leaves my office with the commitment to be in conversation with his dad to learn and understand.

> *"Everything that is in agreement with our personal desires seems true. Everything that is not puts us in a rage."*
>
> ~ André Maurois (n.d.)

Reflect on your relationships, on your interactions with people at work. Let yourself see what views and opinions you are attached to being right about. Let yourself see where you've come at people convincing them to your point of view. Look at the righteousness you have about who you are and how things need to be according to you. Take a Walk on the Inside to explore what is and has been the impact of "being right" on you, on those you love and on others. Discover what it is that you are being "right" about as it relates to your view of each person who is important to you. Discover and uncover the costs for being right about them in the way you are.

What are you arguing for and what is it costing you?

BLAME

At times, life occurs as unfair. Life occurs like life itself, and everyone is against us. Life occurs as hard and difficult, leaving us feeling like we will never have what we want. Each of us, at some point in our lives, faces circumstances that we are whole-heartedly victimized by. Said another way, we believe and we have the experience of "no choice." All of this may be true; and certainly in my own life, I've had experiences and moments of all that I described.

And—so what?

There is no sense of well-being, personal power, and confidence being at the effect of life. In fact, we cultivate disempowerment, powerlessness, and resentment when we blame others for how our life is and how it isn't. We actually keep ourselves small by blaming someone or something else for the conditions and experience of our lives. Yet, blame is inherently part of the human condition. Let's take a closer look, and that is an invitation to see where and with whom you have done the following:

When we perceive someone as being successful, we automatically credit circumstances. It sounds like: "the stars lined up," "they knew the right people," or "market conditions were perfect." Opposite to that is how we automatically blame it on their character when we perceive someone failing. It sounds like: "she is too aggressive," "he is domineering," she is demanding," or "he is meek."

When we perceive ourselves as being successful, we automatically credit our character. It sounds like, "I am passionate," or "I am convincing." When we perceive ourselves to be failing, we automatically blame circumstances. It sounds like, "I didn't get the report on time," or "I was waiting for them to get back to me."

There aren't any actions to take when we are blaming someone or something; we are stuck in victim mentality. Why? Because standing in blame cultivates the underlying belief "I have no power to change anything."

Even when we blame ourselves, we rob ourselves of the ability to take powerful actions to turn the situation around. When we blame ourselves and others, we are most likely making others, ourselves or the situation wrong.

"Anytime we think the problem is out there, that thought is the problem."

~ *Stephen R. Covey (1989, 2004)*

Who and what are you blaming for the conditions of how your life is and how it isn't?

Susan is telling me her husband had an affair about nine years earlier. She talks about the discovery of it, the pain for her, for him and their family. After much conversation, they determined they have more life ahead for them together. They were going to go to counselling to work things out so they could raise their children together. She discloses she is struggling to forgive him.

I ask some questions to learn the kind of work they have done together to restore their connection and trust. I probe to understand the impact her lack of forgiveness has on her, him, their children, and both their family and work lives. I inquire into what happened at the time of the affair, asking her to describe the dynamics of their relationship and communication. She does. As she describes their experience of each other, their marriage, and their life, I hear her blaming him. She is clearly, and naturally so, the victim who has been betrayed. She is angry and hurt, faulting him for all the breakdown, upset, and distance in the relationship leading up to the affair. She walks through events and moments of how it used to be, how it was and how it is now. I hear her sense of powerlessness and her anxiety that she will never get through this. She resists being with all of it. She looks at me and asks, "What can I do?"

I reach across the table and hold her hands in mine. I ask her, "How did you contribute to Grant turning away from you and having the affair?"

There is only her and I; the world around us fades. She looks bewildered. I hold eye contact. I am with her—loving her; present to the privilege it is to be with her innermost fears and heartbreak. I imagine she is moving through lots of spaces and emotions as she chews on my question. I see her courage. I picture her willing to make herself available to seeing what she did and didn't do that had him turn to another woman. I hold the invitation open for her to let go of blaming him and step into acknowledging and owning her contribution to this painful experience. I envision her forgiving him and forgiving herself, giving up forever holding it against him that he hurt her…giving up forever holding it against herself.

It's a big ask, and it's the only way I know that she will ever find peace for herself. I want that for her; otherwise it will eat her up. The trajectory their relationship is on is predictable—divorce. Eventually she says, "I don't know."

"Thank you for being honest. Are you willing to keep looking?" I ask.

She says, "I don't know." We agree to meet again in three weeks.

Susan didn't give up blaming Grant for almost another year. Today, she acknowledges during that time she increasingly became aware of her recurring complaints, growing bitterness, and resentment. She had nurtured her blame for ten years. She was trapped as a victim; miserable. Grant's apologies and remorse made no difference as she stood in being right about him being the villain. No one could shift this situation except her. The day she confronted that, she says to me, "Ask me again how I contributed to Grant turning outside of our marriage to get his needs met." In that moment, Susan stopped blaming, altering her life and her experience of herself, of Grant. She is now in a "new" world.

Blame and fault go hand in hand, founded on the belief of right or wrong. If we are wrong, we blame and criticize ourselves, which actually anchors us in the very behaviour we would like to stop or change. In the face of the inherent need to be right, most often we shine the light on others as being wrong and therefore at fault.

"When you find yourself on a vicious cycle, for goodness sakes, stop pedaling."
~ Steve Bhaerman, a.k.a Swami Beyondananda (2009)

What impact is "blaming" others having on you, and on them?

RESENTMENT

"Resentment is like drinking rat poison and wanting someone else to die."

~ Unknown (n.d.)

The history of a relationship is a mix of joys and hurts, wins and breakdowns, closeness and distance; the list goes on. As indicated above, our inherent need to be right—the automaticity in blaming and making others wrong—creates an impact that most often is not addressed in ways that restore the health of the relationship. Our history with people includes things left unsaid, judgments, and experiences of being hurt —big and small. These often are incomplete conversations we build resentment around, carrying all that past into the present moment and in the future.

We let topics grow into "things" we can't talk about; particularly with sensitive issues such as sex, money, and intimacy. In addition to this, we have expectations, both known and not known, of ourselves and others. These expectations are most often unfulfilled and are a source of friction and suffering, leaving us dissatisfied, isolated, and wanting.

We pretend, with ourselves, with certain people, and with certain matters. We say one thing while thinking the opposite; therefore, being incongruent in our word, thought, and action. This is what it is to be inauthentic.

Another common occurrence in relationship that results in resentment is "with-holding." We with-hold our authentic feelings out of fear of being vulnerable. We'll have very good reasons to justify with-holding, and naturally we make those reasons about the other person rather than ourselves. We have reasons not to engage, not to create and fulfill on what it is we really want, and we'll put it on them. It sounds like, "I/We can't 'x' because he/she is 'y'" (controlling, aggressive, hurtful, closed-minded, angry, etc.).

Familiarity breeds contempt. We are hardest on, and most critical of, those closest to us. We get hurt and we hurt those we love. Human beings can be very unforgiving, remembering the hurts, keeping score, and holding grudges. The conversations we have and don't have when we're hurt often don't bring closure and completion. All of this history becomes the baggage between us and another; and it is some version of resentment.

It's June 2004, and I'm participating in a workshop called, "LifePath™," led by Phil Mittertreiner. I am there to learn how to match my career to my life purpose. The program is designed to increase self-awareness, provide clarity on career direction, and increase personal responsibility to match career choices with strengths. I'm playing full-out in the exercises, leading me to remember a defining moment when I was eight years old.

I'm with my sister Diane, talking to Mrs. Gaudet. I say to Mrs. Gaudet, "The bruises on Diane's face are from her falling down the stairs last night." Mrs. Gaudet looks at me, she looks at Diane, and she looks back at me. She doesn't say a word. I need her to say it will be okay; that we'll be okay. I need her to pat my hand to reassure me. She doesn't. I think to myself, "When I grow up, I'm going to help people talk better."

Again, the already existing unknown shapes my life. My passion for communication is sourced from the moment where I needed Mrs. Gaudet to say something and she didn't. I now make "known" the "unknown." The power of my decision as an eight-year-old is the background of my choices and my career path.

As I reflect on my career, I realize I have dedicated my whole life to helping people talk better. It's been the very nature of my work, in some form or another, for almost my whole career: as a sales representative and trainer for the Dale Carnegie organization, as a sales representative in oil and gas, as a leader and mentor in my various communities, and even as a volunteer. I now understand my passion for communication and my appetite to have people and myself be effective communicators.

While I appreciate my passion born from that moment, I am confronted by my need to be told we were going to be okay. I resent Mrs. Gaudet for what she didn't say, I resent her for doing nothing, and I resent that she didn't give me what I needed. After all, I was eight, and Diane was nine; Mrs. Gaudet was the adult. Aren't adults supposed to take care of the kids? I don't deal with the resentment, as I am righteous about my resentment. Of course it's normal for me to be resentful. At this time, I have no understanding of the impact resentment has on me, my life, and my relationships.

I also didn't consider there was another way to view that life experience. My righteousness is in the way of considering there are alternatives. I didn't know about and nor did I consider I could dissolve resentment. I didn't have any knowledge of tools that could help me shift; and I wasn't looking.

You can learn more about the workshop, "LifePath ™" at www.potentials-unlimited.com.

I'm in Houston, furthering my credentials under the guidance of Dr. John Demartini. He asks us to pick a person we resent or a situation where we are not at peace. Immediately I think of Mrs. Gaudet. I go through Dr. Demartini's process to cause a shift in my view. I do the work; it's not easy work. I'm looking to see what it is I'm not seeing about Mrs. Gaudet and what she did and didn't do. There it is: I recognize that, perhaps from her shoes, saying nothing was the safest thing she could do for us. For the first time in my life, I consider the situation through her eyes. I distinguish for myself that my righteousness and resentment were only limiting me. I see my resentment has had an impact on my health and well-being as well as on my relationships. In shifting my view, I appreciate the difficult position she was in. I shift into being grateful for all that happened and didn't happen the day I spoke to Mrs. Gaudet.

What would your experience of life—yourself and relationships—be if you gave up resentment?

RESISTANCE

The moment we want a situation or a person, including ourselves, to be different from what it is, we are in resistance. It is not possible to be accepting while one is resisting anything, whether it's a quality, action/behaviour, or circumstance. Resistance is a version of being non-accepting. Resistance produces the experience of "not being at peace." Wishing, wanting, needing someone or something to be other than how it is, results in fighting against life. It is impossible to be free when we are resisting someone or something.

Where are you resisting life?

I remember the moment I decided I would never be like my mother.

I'm 11 years old and I'm in the kitchen where mom is, at the counter. She's angry, really angry, and I don't know why she is so angry. I feel it is my fault. I don't know what I've done wrong, and I'm sure I've done something wrong to make her so angry. As I stand there confused and scared, I have the memory of my grandmother's funeral. I was so afraid. I remember how hard I cried, and how I couldn't stop crying when she died a few years earlier. I remember wondering who was going to protect me from my mom's anger. Mom's voice pulls me back to the present moment as she says, "What is wrong with you?" In that moment, I decide I will never be like my mother.

Again, this was an unknown already existing in my background that I did not remember. Living life from a place of "not" costs us energy, happiness, love, and affinity. Living life from a place of "not" actually assures we'll be anchored to the very ways of being and acting we are resisting.

I remember the moment I realized I was exactly like my mother.

I'm 31 years old, married with a two-year-old son who is energetic, beautiful, and happy. It's just before 6:30 in the morning; I'm lying on the couch and Robbie is playing around me. I close my eyes for a moment, when

I feel him tug at me and hear the word "mommy." Almost immediately, I am aware of the familiar little black balls in my feet growing bigger as they course up through my legs and into the pit of my stomach.

It's an all-too-familiar feeling of anger on the edge of losing control. It's an exaggerated level of anger gripping me that I don't understand. I breathe—a long, slow, deep breath—endeavouring to win over the anger. Minutes pass; I am working so hard to breathe and not give myself to my rage. Robbie is tugging harder and getting louder. I remain still with my eyes closed, praying I don't lose to the emotion. The pull to explode as I am consumed by a bigger black rolling ball of fury occurs insurmountable. I stay with my breath while saying "Mommy needs a few minutes." Wait, breathe, breathe, breathe. The storm is passing, I'm winning; the ball of rage is dissolving, I'm relaxing with a sense of calm and gratitude for the win, this time. I open my eyes to see Robbie—beautiful, happy, innocent, and perfect. I am aware of all the times I haven't won over the rage, and how Robbie gets the brunt of that. How when I lose my power to the anger, I blame him and take it out on him. I think to myself, I have this amazing little boy and I am angry all the time. This is the moment I see that I am exactly like my mother. This is the moment I, once again, Take a Walk on the Inside.

Resistance requires a lot of energy, and what we give energy to grows. I want to make sure I have your attention on this point. The point is, I was living inside of a decision I made as an 11-year-old, now distinguished; the "unknown already existing" becomes "known." Now known, I can see the decision to "not" be a certain way anchored me to that way of being within me. I was not at peace, I was not accepting, and I certainly was not free. The experience was of anxiety, criticism, and judgment everywhere and with everyone, and in particular with my mom.

Now known, I now have the space to be at peace, the space to be accepting, and the space to be free. It's important to recognize that peace, acceptance, and freedom do not automatically replace the resistance. My pattern of resistance, resulting in a lack of peace and freedom, as well as being non-accepting, tied me to a certain view and therefore reaction. The views and emotional reactions are ingrained in my brain; my past is automatically there, by default. Now distinguished, I have space; and therefore I've created room to choose how I show up. This requires personal mastery to live "newly" outside of the patterns I have created.

How would the quality of your life be impacted if you were to shift your attention from what you don't want to what you do want?

CONTEXT

"The story I live is created by the story I tell myself."

~ *Abraham Hicks (n.d.)*

The stories we tell ourselves originate from defining moments in childhood, early teen, and adult life. I refer to them as defining moments, given the impact they have on shaping who we become for ourselves and how we view the world. Said another way, in that moment, we make a decision about ourselves; one which is made up, yet so real as it's the way to make sense of what happened. Our decisions become our beliefs as we live into them, eventually forgetting we ever made the decisions— and in many instances forgetting the defining moments. This is the material that becomes the "unknown" already existing. This is what becomes our context: shaping, colouring, and defining our life and our world.

I'm on the phone for a weekly coaching call, sharing with Joy that maybe I've had a dozen dates in the last nine years. I say to Joy, "I'm wondering what is going on with me. I actually believe I'm a pretty good catch. I'm fit, great with people, friendly, approachable, and optimistic. I have a variety of interests, I'm successful in my own business, and I'm financially stable. I rarely get asked out, and hardly ever is there a second date. I really don't understand; and I really want to know what is going on with me."

As Joy poses questions to me and we explore my paradigm about men, dating, love, and me, I discover several blind spots. I discover that who I am for myself is a failure at love. In other words, I believe I'm a failure at love. Fundamentally, I hold the view that men are dangerous. Although I speak about wanting a committed relationship, I realize I have a wall around my heart and I'm actually unavailable to anyone. Digging deeper,

I confront a core belief I have about myself—I'm unlovable.

Joy asks, "What are your payoffs in keeping all of this alive?" I think, I look, and I sit with all the stuff I've uncovered with compassion for myself and my own humanity. What a gold mine. I have hope and power, recognizing that now I acknowledge it authentically, I can transform my thinking and this area of my life. What are the payoffs? I realize I am keeping myself safe from being hurt—again. I get to hide the ugliness and emptiness I feel on the inside, founded on the belief I am unlovable and unworthy of a great relationship. I grasp how I have it rigged so I don't have to be vulnerable. I recognize my attachment to being fiercely independent, which protects me, or so I tell myself. I identify both fear and contempt for the idea of being needy.

I am in a state of "Wow, really wow! Who would want to date all that?" Now that I am conscious of my story about men, dating, love, and me; it's no surprise I've been single most of my life. All of my beliefs, and filters are made up, based on past moments and decisions. My context is the already existing and it isn't known to me until I Take a Walk on the Inside in the area of intimate love and partnership.

So what? Knowing all of that makes no difference. Knowing all of that doesn't alter the existing patterns, beliefs, and ways of being. Knowing all of that about myself doesn't create opportunities for me to have intimate love and a great relationship in my life.

Now what? Now that I've distinguished my paradigm in the area of intimate love and partnership, I can put all of that aside. Putting it aside is a moment-by-moment phenomenon. Once I put it all aside, I am now standing in a clean space—pure potential—where I can paint a new picture; create a new possibility in this area of life. I create and declare the possibility of "exquisite love and partnership that lasts a lifetime." I have no idea how to fulfill this possibility, nor do I have any grasp on what it will take of me to fulfill it. What I do have is anticipation, excitement, and a new future. I have the experience of personal power. I now have my word in the matter, I have a say, a real say in how my life in the area of intimate love and partnership is going to go. I am present to magic and wonder, living into the possibility of exquisite love and partnership that lasts a lifetime.

What is your picture of living a life you love?

The Decisions:

I'm standing at the top of the stairs, at eight years old, watching my mom and my step-dad beat my nine-year-old sister Diane. I've taken several walks on the inside, over my lifetime, to distinguish the far-reaching impact and decisions that I as an eight-year old made. This was the story of my life; I was ruled by the decisions that eight-year-old made. Still today, in moments when I am gripped by my past, it is the story of my life.

I am screaming at them to stop, with tears streaming down my face. They don't. I couldn't stop them. Decision: There is something wrong with me. Decision: It's my fault. Decision: I am not enough. Decision: People need to be saved.

Diane is being held down, and there is a moment where the look in her eyes is one of a deer taking its final breath. Decision: No one will ever control me. Decision: Men are dangerous.

It's my mom and step-dad, raging. Decision: You can't count on people, even family. Decision: Family is a burden. Decision: Love isn't safe. Decision: Needing someone isn't safe.

As my step-dad comes up the stairs and approaches me, he yells, "Why are you crying"? I say, "I'm scared." What I remember him saying is, "Don't ever be like her and this won't happen to you." Decision: Be anything and do anything other than be like Diane.

> *"How often do we stand convinced of the truth of our early memories, forgetting that they are assessments made by a child? We can replace the narratives that hold us back by inventing wiser stories, free from childish fears, and, in doing so, disperse long-held psychological stumbling blocks."*
>
> *~ Benjamin Zander, The Art of Possibility (2002)*

What are you now seeing that you could not see before?

We talk ourselves into and out of actions every day. What we do and don't do is ruled by our context. The decisions become our context— the filters and lenses through which we see and experience the world.

Do I have that conversation with my boss or not?

Do I eat that piece of chocolate cake or not?

Do I forgive my sister/husband/mother/father/brother/friend or not?

Do I buy that or not?

*I'm watching the workshop leader Angie work with a young woman about some history with her dad. At Angie's instructions, there are participants playing the roles of mom, sister, step-mom, dad, and dad's best friend. Angie asks the girl, "What would your dad's best friend think about your dad?" The moment stands still for me. I see the lens through which I see my dad. The view I have of my dad is that he **is** the bad guy. I pick up my phone, step out of the room, and phone my dad.*

Dad says "Hello," and I say "Hi, Dad. I'm in a workshop and I just saw something about my relationship with you."

Dad says, "What's that?"

I express, ever so softly, "I realize that even at our closest times, like when I left Denis and you drove to Calgary every couple of weeks to check in on the kids and me, I have you as the bad guy." I wait. My 77-year-old father is sobbing. I wait. "I'm sorry, Dad. I didn't realize I had you as the bad guy. I'm committed you have the experience of being unconditionally loved." He thanks me, and we say good-bye.

> *"You see everything is about belief, whatever we believe rules our existence, rules our life."*
>
> ~ Don Miguel Ruiz, The Four Agreements (1997)

It's how we think about situations and ourselves that has us do or not do something. Each of us has a unique network of filters impacting what we see and hear, and how we behave, show up, and interact. The filters, both known and unknown, that we operate through, are what is called our "context." Context is made of up layers of filters shaping, colouring and defining how we see ourselves and others and how we experience life. The filters are sourced by our past, ideas, and beliefs we inherit from our families, religions, and culture, and views we bought into from society—both known and unknown. Our context is a combination of personal experiences, beliefs, attitudes, decisions, opinions, biases, and prejudices; again, both known and unknown.

Context is omnipresent; it is like what air is to a bird or what water is to a fish. Context is just the way life is, the way we are, and just the way life is going to go; it appears as real and unchangeable. For human beings, context appears real, as the truth. As such, we rarely challenge how we think about ourselves, others and situations—it's just the way life is. Context is decisive—pervasive—influencing everything: what we do and don't do, what we hear and don't hear, what we see and don't see, what we think and what we don't know we think. Our experiences, the very quality of our lives, are determined by our context.

"...you created your home movies of various patterns of interaction in your family. Your parents' role in setting those patterns is central, and their relationship has affected you from your roots to the present.... As you grew, your understanding of yourself was primarily determined by your parents' actions." (Foster, 1993, p.56)

What are some of the patterns and beliefs you inherited?

Dean says, "I'd like to work in the family business."

I ask, "Why don't you?"

He says, "I've never told my dad, or anyone I want to. I don't feel like I can ask for that."

"What happened, Dean?"

"When I was seventeen, I was out in the yard helping dad. We were arguing and I blurted out, don't ever ask me for help again! I left him there. I feel so guilty. I let him down over nothing; so stupid."

I say, "That was nineteen years ago."

He looks at me with sorrow, shame, and hurt, and says, "I know—I just couldn't ask to be part of the business because of that. I have no right to."

In a family retreat, Dean apologizes to his dad for his outburst, sharing the impact it had on him. In doing so, he forgives himself, relieving himself of the burden of guilt and shame he's been carrying for so long. Dean's dad did not remember that event at all. Imagine the time and energy wasted; and the far-reaching impact. Dean's dream abandoned and perhaps his dad wondering why Dean has never expressed an interest in working in the family business. This is both the power and impact of context!

Each person's context is unique, which explains why we can all be listening or watching the same thing, yet all hear and see something slightly different. I've included the following excerpt from *Fierce Conversations* (2004) as I didn't think I could say it better or clearer:

> "It is not so difficult to understand how misunderstandings and conversational fly-bys occur, given that each of us experiences life in a unique context—a filter consisting of our strongly held opinions, beliefs, and attitudes, which has been shaped and reinforced over a lifetime. Our context determines how we experience the content of our lives. Often our context takes the form of rules to live by…. Each individual has his or her context and lives his or her life accordingly. It gets interesting when the content in our lives includes the meaning and intent of every conversation in which we participate. And therefore, the outcomes. Remember, all conversations are with myself, and sometimes they involve other people. This is true in the sense that we all unconsciously, automatically put our own interpretation or spin on the words of others. We are all constantly interpreting everything we hear others say. And constantly being interpreted, in turn." (Scott, 2004, pp. 179–180)

AUTOMATICITY IN BEING HUMAN

Consider how much of your day and my day—in fact, every human being's day—is spent operating on autopilot. The things we do without thinking. The things we say without thinking. The things we see without thinking.

Yes, you do say and see things without thinking.

What will it take to disrupt your patterned ways of thinking and seeing the world?

"Thinking is the hardest work there is, which is probably the reason why so few engage in it."

~ Henry Ford (n.d.)

Our brain is designed for survival; developing and using patterns to conserve energy. It is this design that preserves the patterns, repeats activities and keeps us operating on autopilot most of the time.

PATTERNS AND TRIGGERS

…Most of the time your brain is involved in just one of three activities: distraction, reaction or following well-worn patterns…. Your mind consistently chooses to follow well-worn patterns rather than generate new thoughts, new interpretations or new ways of doing things. Human beings are wired to live in and from old patterns, said another way emotional memories rather than thinking new thoughts…. pattern recognition has been and continues to be one of our most important survival mechanisms. Our patterns are like tethers constantly pulling us back to the known, the familiar, the safe. (Hurson, 2008, pp. 19, 23)

It's January 2015, and I'm in Dubai, participating in a leadership course at Zayed University. We are told in the leadership course that neuroscience says about 80 percent of what we see is seen by the patterns in our brain, versus seeing what is actually in front of us. It was, and is still, startling to me to hear that neuroscience research shows 80 percent or more of what we see is generated by pre-existing patterns in the brain (Erhard, Jensen, Zaffron & Echeverria, 2008).

In addition to the fact that most of what we see is created by pre-existing patterns, we also know that less than 10 percent of the mind is conscious.

Think about that: 5 percent of the mind is conscious, struggling against the 95 percent that is running subconscious automatic programs. We've memorized a set of behaviors so well that we have become an automatic, habitual body-mind. In fact, when the body has memorized a thought, action or feeling to the extent that the body is the mind—when mind and body are one—we are (in a state of) being the memory of ourselves. And if 95 percent of who we are by age 35 is a set of involuntary programs, memorized behaviors, and habitual emotional reactions, it follows that 95 percent of our day, we are unconscious. We only appear to be awake. Yikes! (Dispenza, 2012, pp. 62-63)

Enough about the brain.

The very nature of context cultivates automaticity; that is, our autopilot mode or default patterns. These patterns are embedded in our context—in our ways of being, seeing, acting, and communicating. We are prisoners of our context; it limits what is possible for us until we consciously recognize it. Being aware of our story is key as the first step towards freedom; and, as with many things, knowing makes no difference.

I get into bed, moving close to Tim. He is reading, as he often does. He doesn't look up or move closer to snuggle with me. My first thought is, "I am not welcome; he doesn't want me." I have a swirling emotional experience on the inside, my body is tensing up, and I am afraid. I don't say anything. I lay there stiffly beside him, quietly suffering and building my negative experience. He continues to read. A short time passes, he puts the book down, turns off the light, and kisses me goodnight. We each roll over, with our backs to each other. I have the experience of being rejected. Now I am trapped with an escalating storm brewing on the inside. When I can't stand the internal turmoil anymore, I finally say, "I don't feel welcome here." He turns on the light, moves close to me and tenderly says, "What do you need right now?" Emotions and thoughts are churning and racing, none of which I can settle. I sit up, declaring "I have to go!" I'm out of bed, I have my clothes on, bag in hand, and I'm at the door putting on my coat, moving at an unstoppable pace and momentum.

I am not choosing; I am once again gripped by my past. I know I'm triggered and I know what triggered me. I know this man loves me. I know my old context and default patterns have a hold on me. I know I'm in survival mode—surviving my old context that men are dangerous, I'm a failure at love, and needing someone is risky. In this moment, knowing makes no difference.

He is with me, watching me and very much wanting the outcome to be different. It's clear, my decision is made; only it's not my decision as in present tense. The decision to leave is based on my default way of being triggered into survival mode. I am in my car, on my way home at midnight, upset and alone. He is alone, left with the impact of my triggers and automaticity of the context I, as an eight-year-old girl, made up.

This is what it is to be human. We all know this human experience. It is referred to as the "amygdala hijack," a phrase coined by Daniel Goleman in his work on *Emotional Intelligence* (2005). It is the amygdala in our brain that regulates our fight or flight response. When threatened, it hijacks us with an emotional response.

What are the recurring triggers and conversations in your relationships?

This kind of experience, common to all of us, can be the inspiration to courageously Take a Walk on the Inside. These repeated experiences are why I put together my own suite of elements for Personal Mastery.

It's now almost a year since I've been living in Red Deer, and I'm on the phone with Denis. He is my former boyfriend, whom I dated for a year when I lived in Lloydminster. Denis decided he didn't want a long-distance relationship, and discontinued our relationship when I left Lloydminster. We talked occasionally as friends, although I was pretending to be okay with being "just friends." I was never just his friend—I love him; I believe I'm going to marry him. I have it; he is my soul-mate.

I say to Denis, "I got a job in Calgary, and I'm moving next month." Denis replies, "Congratulations, Trudy." The next words I hear are, "I will marry you when you earn fifty-thousand dollars." Although he was joking, I take his words to heart. I love this man; and now I know exactly what to do in order for him to love me. I kick into action, and guess what: I set out to earn $50,000, because this is how I get to be loved. Only, I don't recognize my past is running me. I don't recognize I am triggered and my context has kicked into automatic.

This is completely aligned with my strategy to "earn love," only I don't remember that I created that strategy as the way for me to be loved. At nine years old, I'm sitting at the supper table with my family. I look at each of them: my sister Diane is the beautiful one, my brother is the only boy, and my sister Lela is the baby. I have no special talent or beauty. I am the second oldest, in the shadow of my siblings, and I look like my dad, which apparently isn't good news.

I'm looking at them and thinking to myself, I really don't belong. I wonder, how could I belong? What can I do to belong? What can I do in order to matter—to be loved? I see it. I know exactly what to do; in fact, I have already experienced approval for being helpful. I decide I'm going to make a place for myself in this family and get love and approval by doing things for people. It makes perfect sense to me—do things for others. Do things for others so they will love me. Do things so they will approve of me. Do things so I belong.

It begins. I'm the first up from the table to start cleaning up. I'm the first up and outside to milk the cows and feed the chickens each morning. I'm the first up on Saturday morning, firing up the vacuum cleaner to vacuum the floors. I help with building fences, cooking, weeding the garden, making lunches. DO – DO – DO is my strategy in order to belong, in order to be loved and approved of. It works. I remember my siblings calling me the pet. I am the pet. I remember the resentment I sense from them, and it doesn't matter because this is how I get to matter to my parents. The harder I work, the more approval, love, and sense of belonging I have.

Denis's words are innocent and in the end, such a gift to me. I would not have discovered this context, the unknown already existing, if I had not been triggered into the automaticity of doing. It isn't long before I am earning $50,000, and shortly after I meet that target, we are married. All of which validate for me that there really is something wrong with me, I am unworthy of love and I don't belong. Working hard and "doing" for others is the only way I can earn and therefore deserve love, and it's the only way I will ever belong.

What are your triggers that kick you into automatic?

While most of my stories focus on the downside of the decisions I made as a young girl, I am also present to the strengths and positive qualities I developed. The strengths I developed as a result of the decisions I made in of those defining moments are invaluable and contributed to my success and achievement in life. I am a self-starter, self-reliant, driven, passionate, and quick to take action. I am intuitive, a perceptive listener with a "people-smart" ability. I am a visionary, trustworthy and expressive.

I now understand how my strengths can grip me in the same way my limiting and negative beliefs do. The saying "overused strengths become our weaknesses" has certainly been true of me. There have been, and still are, times when I have been run by the very strengths I've developed even though I or the situation would have been better served to show up differently; other than in my strong suits.

Nonetheless, I would not trade any of what has happened in my life and I can appreciate the decisions I made as a result of specific defining moments.

What are your strengths and the qualities in yourself that you admire and appreciate?

What are the defining moments and decisions that is the source of them?

REACTION — AT THE EFFECT OF CIRCUMSTANCES

"When a human being is pushed, that human being pushes back."

~ *Trudy Pelletier*

Life is a roller coaster; and if we answer the question "How often do we actually enjoy the ride?" Honestly, many of us—and certainly all of us in moments and for periods of time—would say we don't enjoy the ride. We live like a feather blowing in the wind surviving people, ourselves, and life. Many humans are living life as though something is happening to us and actually not remembering that we have the power to create our life; and, going further, being responsible for creating our life as it is and as it isn't.

What is your experience of life?

How does life occur for you?

As I reflect on my life and my work with others as they've shared some of their most intimate and personal experiences and aspirations, I see how much of life is a reaction. Reaction to pressures and worry, constant comparison, competition, and survival mode. Reaction to decisions to never do or be a certain way... Reaction by pushing back... Reaction to the experience of being powerless...

I'm about to step on the scale and take my measurements for myself and my accountability partner in the health and fitness program I've committed to for three months. I am already anxious at the thought of knowing the numbers. I put so much meaning and significance on the numbers that the critical internal conversation already has me on guard. It doesn't matter I'm feeling strong and lean. It doesn't matter that yesterday I received a beautiful compliment. It doesn't matter that I've engaged in the program with 100 percent integrity. If the numbers aren't a match to all of that, everything is discounted. I'm at the effect of the numbers.

Taking a Walk on the Inside to meet myself gives me the opportunity to recognize and own my network of beliefs; the stories and decisions I made up. I get to uncover and discover where I've limited myself, where my past is running my life based on those defining moments and decisions I made about myself and my life when I was very young. I confront the perception that while it occurs as though it's real, none of it is real. I allow myself to see and transform, to live life on purpose.

In what situations are you living at the effect of circumstances?

"It's not what happens to you, but how you react to it that matters."

~ *Epictetus (n.d.)*

I am leaving Safeway with a bag of groceries in hand when I see a woman struggling with a very full cart, a baby on her hip and a little girl holding her hand. With the intention she is freed up to take care of her children, I ask her if I can walk her cart out to her car for her. I think my offer surprises her and she immediately responds, "We can manage." I persist by saying "I'd be happy

60

to help" and she answers "No." As I walk away, she says, "Thanks anyway." Her reaction was immediate; I felt she did not allow for the possibility to receive.

As I consider my experience with her, I wonder what is the "unknown, already existing." Then I remember a time in my life when I would not and could not accept help. I simply had the belief accepting help meant I was weak. I see that I was in reaction all the time; proving I'm strong, demonstrating my fierce independence. It is the "known, already existing" that is playing out in my reactions to any offer of help or kindness.

If you were to pick an area of life that isn't working as well as you would like, and let yourself discover what it is that you can't see, what would you see?

IS / AM

> *"Once you label me you negate me."*
>
> ~ Søren Kierkegaard (n.d.)

What are the labels you give yourself?

Judging and labelling is inherent in human beings, and we live as though the labels we give ourselves and others are true. The labels we live into as the "truth" become the "way we are" and the "way others are"; said another way, "unchangeable." The labels occur as permanent, speaking about ourselves and others as an object or a thing. We objectify others, our world and even ourselves. The definition of objectify is "to present as an object, make objective; externalize; to represent concretely." (www.dictionary.com, 2016)

It's 2007 in Houston, and I'm in a class with Dr. John Demartini, being trained in the Demartini Method®, the Breakthrough Experience®. I am enthralled with his work, specifically the idea that everything is in perfect balance all the time and that is the true way of nature. What I understand from his work is that there are both pros and cons in everything (situations/ experiences/qualities). When we resist or reject qualities in ourselves or others, we are seeing only one side of things, which actually creates a barrier to seeing anything else. In other words, if we are labelling a quality as bad, most likely we have an emotional charge around it, so we can only see it as bad. We become polarized in the view of "it's bad," and that stops us from seeing it any other way. His work is designed to remove emotional charges and triggers when we resist something in ourselves or in other people.

*Our assignment is to take a quality we reject in ourselves or a significant person in our life. I decide I'm going to deal with my intensity. I've received so much feedback, all negative, over so many years that I know for certain I have to deal with this. **I have been labelled as intense and so who I am is intense.** Being intense is not a positive way of being; it's a really bad thing. I go to work on the assignment. To my delight, I discover all the upside about being intense. Discovery enables a person to be balanced (no longer emotionally charged) seeing both the pros and cons. This frees people to choose when they are intense or not. The shift gives the ability to choose that one can be intense or one can be relaxed.*

"What's important is that we maintain our illusion of the world as concrete, rational, and predictable." (Hurson, 2008, p.55)

What we human beings do is label. We label and we are not aware of the labels we assign. There is the emotional history with family members, such that we hold an automatic view and/or reoccurring experience of each of them. In my work with business families, when I ask the questions:

Who is your dad for you?

Who is your mom for you?

Who is your sister for you?

Who is your brother for you?

These are questions that cause a pause. Perplexed, confused, and shaken, my clients confront the labels they have assigned family members and how that makes them just the way they are. They see how their labels has them be a "certain way"; and that certain way is just who they are.

What are the labels you have assigned others that are barriers to love and affinity?

POSSIBILITIES

> *"In the measurement world, you set a goal and strive for it. In the universe of possibility, you set the context and let life unfold."*
>
> *~ Benjamin Zander, The Art of Possibility (2002)*

This is an invitation for you to create a context for possibilities such that you believe it's possible for you to have anything you want for yourself and your life.

The definition of "possible" is

1. That may or can be, exist, happen, be done, be used, etc.

2. That may be true or may be the case, as something concerning which one has no knowledge to the contrary

3. Capable of existing, taking place, or proving true without contravention of any natural law

4. Capable of being achieved: it is not possible to finish in three weeks

5. Having potential or capabilities for favourable use or development: the idea is a possible money-spinner (www.dictionary.com, 2016)

We must first distinguish what your context is for what's possible. There will be ideas and beliefs you "know" about what's possible, and there will be ideas and beliefs in the background, what I've described as the "unknown, already existing." You are looking for the multi-dimensions coupled with the whole range of thoughts about miracles and magic, as well as the limiting thoughts that has you be resigned and cynical.

What do you think and believe is possible for you?

Look deeper.

What do you really think and believe is possible for you?

Answer the same questions in each area of life.

Career – Finances – Health and Fitness – Family – Community – Spirituality – Social Network – Learning and Development

I invite you to explore and discover what your internal conversation is in the background when you read:

-You can have it all.

-You can be happy.

-You can be rich.

-You can be fulfilled.

-You are unlimited in what you can be, do, and have.

-You can have anything you want for yourself and your life.

Every time I Take a Walk on the Inside, I discover limiting thoughts and ideas, thus giving me "new" space to create a possibility. I am free to create any possibility I want for myself and my life inside of that new space. Standing in that, all there is for me to do is to become reliable through Personal Mastery to keep that possibility alive, making it my reality moment-by-moment. That's life: moment-by-moment. Now! And Now! And Now!

I've shared several of the possibilities throughout this book that I've created.

The possibility of:

-An upset free life

-Exquisite love and partnership that lasts a lifetime

-Being accomplished

-Being lovable and worthy

As human beings, we don't wake up with our possibilities (dreams and aspirations); we wake up with our worries and concerns. In many instances, we settle for less in the face of the tension produced by what we want and what we are experiencing. Personal Mastery is my access and I share it with you with the intention that you live an extraordinary life of possibilities.

What is possible for you that up until now you have considered impossible for you?

This, therefore, is a faded dream of a time when I went down into the dust and noise of the eastern marketplace. And with my brain and muscles, with sweat and constant thinking, made others see my dreams come true. Those who dream by night in the dusty recesses of their minds, wake in the day to find all that was vanity; but the dreamers of the day are dangerous men, for they may act their dreams with open eyes and make it possible.

~ *T. E. Lawrence (n.d.)*

3. How?

LEADERSHIP

"If you are not consciously directing your life, you will lose your footing and circumstances will decide for you."

~ Michael Bernard Beckwith (n.d.)

When most people think about leadership, they normally think about leading others. I mean something different. I mean self-directed leadership, which is not the kind of leadership we automatically think about when we hear or read "leadership." The automatic thinking about leadership is "leading others." The emphasis is on leading others, and although it may assume it includes leading oneself, it isn't written or spoken of.

The dictionary definition of leadership is as follows: "The position or function of a leader, a person who guides or directs a group; ability to lead; an act or instance of leading; guidance; direction; the leaders of a group" (www.dictionary.com, 2016).

I'm left wondering what difference it would make to our teams, companies, communities, and world if the first thought on leadership was being self-directed. What I mean is when we think about leadership, we first look at ourselves. The discipline to look at ourselves to consider our role in / contribution to the results we and our teams have produced. What most leaders do is look at others, point to others, lay blame and look for fault in others.

Self-directed leadership is having a command over self in ways that have us deal with the circumstances of life powerfully, effectively, and deliberately. This means an ever growing capacity to be responsible— able to respond to life on all levels and in all ways.

What impact would you have if you stepped into self-directed leadership?

"Life isn't about finding yourself. Life is about creating yourself."

~ George Bernard Shaw (n.d.)

WAIT AND SEE

I'm facilitating a private Fierce Conversations workshop for a group of seventeen executives. I invite the participants to introduce themselves and their roles, share their biggest leadership challenges, and name two goals they want to accomplish in our two-day workshop. As we move through the room, I'm developing rapport, establishing credibility, and making key points that are foundational to the workshop and opportunities the program offers. The executive vice-president has the floor as he talks through the introduction format I have asked them to use. I'm engaging with questions to clarify and connect, when he responds to my question about his goals with "I'll wait and see." I suggest there would be greater value for him if he named a goal for the program. Again he expresses, "I'm going to wait and see" with a stronger tone.

What would happen if we were trained and developed to first look at ourselves when our team and our organization didn't produce the results we intended and inspired?

In my conversations with colleagues and clients, I see and hear their disappointment in the results in various work and learning events they have participated in. I wonder how often this happens as a result of the "wait and see" attitude. As a facilitator, I see how often people actually put the entire responsibility, for what they will or will not get from our work together on me. It reflects a context that "it's someone else's responsibility for your own learning and growth." It's the expectation, and even belief, that someone else can give it to you or make it happen for you. I often assert there are ample golden opportunities in the conversation, and it's their intentions and goals that determine fulfillment or not.

What would become available to you if you step into leading yourself right now—in any area of life?

LEARNING

"Leadership and learning are indispensable to each other."

~ John F. Kennedy (n.d.)

It's November in Los Angeles, where my friend Janice and I are attending a program created and delivered by Dr. John Demartini called the "Breakthrough Experience". I am there as a result of a reaction to a conversation my dad had with my kids. I'm there to uncover, explore, understand, and discover what goes on when I am triggered. In spite of the significant investment I've made in my personal and spiritual growth, I found myself raging on the inside, full of resentment towards my dad.

Earlier that year, my dad is sitting in my home with my 17-year-old son Robbie and Alicia, my 14-year-old daughter. He says, "I won't be at your graduations and your weddings. I won't be there because I have no desire to ever see your grandmother again." I am angry! Flaring up and hardening on the inside, full of criticism, hurt, and rage. I think, how dare he! I've spent thousands and thousands of dollars on workshops, books, and counselling, on myself to break the cycle. I've invested my heart and soul so my kids would not know the tension of having to choose between family members. I am livid and experiencing an out-of-control wrath towards my dad as I see that he's just asked them to choose between him and their grandmother; and as a result he's having me choose between my mom and my dad.

It might be obvious to you that what dad actually said and what I heard were two different things. Had I calmed down and replayed what he actually said, I would have seen that I interpreted his words differently from what he said. I would have acknowledged that he was actually courageously choosing to not participate in certain family events for his own reasons. It had nothing to do with me and nothing to do with my kids.

I think of the metaphor of the onion; peeling back the layers of the onion is uncovering the layers of the complexities of our beliefs, thoughts, and emotions. I am grateful for that experience with my dad, for that propelled me to expand my learning and understanding of myself. I was introduced to a new world through Demartini's work.

"The highest form of maturity is self-inquiry."

~ Martin Luther King Jr. (n.d.)

I declare I am a lifelong learner. Learning is one of my highest values. At one time, my learning was driven by the "unknown, already existing"— something is wrong with me. Today my learning is sourced by my appetite to discover my "unknown, pure potential."

When was the last time you discovered something new about yourself, and what was it?

PERSONAL MASTERY

"One can have no smaller or greater mastery than mastery of oneself."

~ Leonardo da Vinci (n.d.)

Personal Mastery is not a place we arrive at. It is not a destination nor is it somewhere to get to. Personal Mastery is not a permanent state, nor is it a fixed result. Personal Mastery is not power over another human being, nor is it power over a situation or circumstance.

Personal Mastery is a moment-to-moment state, enabling us to be our "best self" in the face of any circumstance. Personal Mastery is having a command over oneself, particularly when we are triggered. Personal Mastery gives us access to show up congruently and consistently with our values, aspirations, and our word about who we say we are in life. The vision we have for who we are aspiring to become, what we would love to be doing and have, both tangible and intangible.

Personal Mastery is the experience of being responsive when life happens, rather than being reactive when life happens.

It's March 2013, and I'm having lunch with my dad. He blurts out, "Trudy, why can't you keep a man?" I hear criticism. I immediately shrink while thinking, "There is something wrong with me." My heart feels cut—deeply hurt—and my head is reeling. I want to strike back. I want him to hurt as much as I do in this moment. I want him to know what a crappy human being he is. I want to make him wrong. I am triggered and in reaction, reeling emotionally into the dark side of the line.

I breathe, grappling with myself to get balance. I continue to breathe as I tell myself, say nothing. I don't know how much time passes—three seconds, thirty seconds, three minutes. My next thought with my next breath, is, Trudy, he loves you; he's just worried about you. I take another breath, and I can feel my body settling, my heart softening. Another breath, with the thought, you can be great; he just loves you. In the next moment, I say, "Dad, thank you so much for caring for me so very much. I know you love me and you don't want me to be alone."

My dad and I are connected in an experience of love and affinity. Having command over me and my reactions—emotional, mental, and physical—took everything I had to be responsive to my dad, and it might have gone so differently. I have personal power; I'm enjoying the experience of mastery over my reaction. I am congruent and authentic with my dad and with myself, which includes my values, my personal vision, and who I say I am in the world.

> *"No one is free who has not obtained the empire of himself.*
> *No man is free who cannot command himself."*
>
> ~ *Pythagoras (n.d.)*

In *The Fifth Discipline: The Art and Practice of the Learning Organization* (1990), Peter Senge explains:

> Personal mastery is the discipline of continually clarifying and deepening our personal vision, of focusing our energies, of developing patience, and of seeing reality objectively. It goes beyond competence and skills, although it involves them...People with a high level of personal mastery live in a continual learning mode. They never 'arrive.' But personal mastery is not something you possess. It is a process. It is a lifelong discipline. (Senge, 1990, p. 142)

There is a direct link between "Personal Mastery" and fulfillment, contentment, and success, regardless of what your personal definition of success is. This link exists whether your desire is for success in business, health, wealth, relationships, family, or love. It is power founded on commitment and discipline to develop a suite of muscles. Personal mastery is available to each of us on the planet; and it's not for the faint of heart. Building the Personal Mastery muscles will empower you to create yourself as someone who is grounded in the best essence of yourself and what it is to be human.

The following story illustrates how Personal Mastery is only ever "now" —a moment-by-moment phenomenon.

I walk into the car rental office to pick up the vehicle the body shop has arranged for me to drive while my car is in the shop, getting repaired from the hail damage. The young man says, "I have a mini-van that will be out front for you in just a few minutes." I react and say, "The body shop said they arranged for a vehicle comparable to my Acura TSX." The young man says, "I'm sorry, it's the only vehicle I have available." I arrogantly assert, "I have raised two kids and have never driven a mini-van; there's no way I'm leaving here in a mini-van." Tension increases as he says, "I will call some of our other outlets, but I do know how little is available due to the volume of repairs the hail storms have caused." I don't pay attention to him. I want what I want, and I want it how I want it! I'm demanding, harsh, and abrasive. I open my laptop to go to work while I wait. Almost three hours have passed when I realize I have a lunch meeting to go to. I pack up my work, go back to the counter, and proceed to put the young man in his place because he's not produced another vehicle for me to drive.

As I get in the mini-van, I know that I have ruined his day. I was awful. I have the experience of being a small human being for having been so angry and careless. I actually don't like myself at all in this moment.

What impact are you committed to having in—and on—the world?

THE ELEMENTS OF PERSONAL MASTERY

"Always pass on what you have learned."

~Yoda (n.d.)

The elements of Personal Mastery I'm offering you are from my collection from the many walks on the inside I've taken and the numerous discoveries I've made. You may recognize there is nothing new or revolutionary in the elements. I am not saying these are the only elements that may be considered aspects of Personal Mastery and you are limited to these elements. There is a large body of work on mastery and personal mastery out in the world. I invite you to add to your understanding and toolkit to engage in the game of becoming a master. I do assert this is an infinite game with no end. Mastery is not somewhere to arrive at; it is the act of mastering ourselves. Said another way, mastery is reliably having command of yourself in any circumstance.

SELF-AWARENESS

"Until you make the unconscious conscious, it will direct your life and you will call it fate."

~ C.G. Jung (n.d.)

Philosophy and thought leaders across cultures and the ages unanimously agree "self-awareness" is fundamental to living and leading a great life: to be aware of oneself, on all levels, and in all ways. Self-awareness gives us the ability to understand ourselves, all for the purpose of improving the quality of our lives and realizing our potential.

Don is speaking with his business coach Caryn, and she shares, "I'm on a diet." Don looks at her and says, "It doesn't show." She pauses. She sits with his words and her reaction. She lets herself be present to Don; how he shows up and who he is behind the nastiness. She then says, "Who would you be if you weren't nasty?" Don quickly retorts, "You get paid for this coaching?" As Don walks away, he knows he is not the same man who walked into the room. While he doesn't know all the implications, he does know he has fundamentally shifted in who he is for himself.

Years later, Don confesses to Caryn, "In that moment and in the way you asked that question, my self-awareness was awakened, and I became hungry to discover who I was and who I could be."

Choice is a function of awareness. We have more choices to deal with life, people, and circumstances when we are aware of what is happening for us, emotionally, mentally, and physically.

Consider that our primary relationship in life is the one we have with ourselves. Who you are for you, and how you see yourself is directly correlated to the quality of your life. We are alive and engaged in life when we have a healthy and empowering relationship with ourselves.

"You cannot heal what you do not acknowledge."

~ Richard Rohr (n.d.)

There are several practices, approaches and disciplines to expand self-awareness. I've utilized a number of different works, all of which have supported me to become self-aware. This doesn't mean I am aware all the time, as I've shown through sharing some of the "amygdala hijacks" I've had.

I use the role of "observer" to collect data on the human being I am. I deliberately separate myself from my thoughts and feelings. I am not my thoughts; I have thoughts. I am not my feelings; I have feelings. I am not my experiences; I have experiences. Deliberately separating myself from my thoughts, feelings, and experiences so I can collect data creates room for me to better understand my context and therefore me. I use the following questions when I notice myself in reaction, labelling, making wrong, blaming, resisting, and have the experience of being stuck:

-What is it I'm not seeing?

-How could I see this differently?

-What is the opportunity for me in this situation?

Who are you for yourself?

RESPONSIBLE

"Responsibility is a grace I give myself."

~ Unknown (n.d.)

For many of us, the "unknown" already existing definition of "responsible" is blame and fault. This is an inherited definition of the word "responsible" given that we as human beings naturally and automatically make others wrong and assign blame. Someone who has this context will never step into being responsible.

What is your definition (your picture) of "responsible"?

Be straight, as you might respond to the question with the answer that has you look and sound good.

Being responsible is simply a place to live life from. Living life from this place enables us to have a say in how life goes for us. This doesn't mean having control over life. It means having power in life to take action to create a life you love and to make a difference in the areas that really matter to you. Living life by being responsible is a door through which one grows in spirit and capacity. We become bigger when we live from a place of being responsible.

An online dictionary defines "responsible" as:

1. Answerable or accountable, as for something within one's power, control, or management

2. Involving accountability or responsibility, as in having the power to control or manage

3. Chargeable with being the author, cause, or occasion of something

4. Having a capacity for moral decisions and therefore accountable; capable of rational thought or action

5. Reliable or dependable, as in meeting debts, conducting business dealings, etc. (www.dictionary.com, 2016)

It's been 11 years since I have seen Marilyn, and now I am sitting at her kitchen table. It took me a week to find her through social media. In my heart of hearts, I have known for years that I owe her an apology. It's taken me that long to acknowledge that knowing within me. I don't know why it's taken me so long given the relief I am experiencing just sitting with her. I am so thankful she has agreed to see me. We catch up on our lives, anticipating the "real" conversation we both know is long overdue. Courageously I offer, "I came to apologize to you. I know our work environment wasn't conducive to being a team and supporting each other. I recognize I was competitive and driven to the point of sacrificing a relationship with you. I was nasty. I am not here to blame anyone. I am here to own it, to acknowledge it, and to apologize to you. I have done you an injustice. You didn't deserve to be treated so poorly. I am deeply sorry."

She looks at me and simply says, "Thank you." There is nothing more to say. We are complete, both of us restored to peace. I discover the power from being responsible and cleaning things up, and in that moment I am free.

What is your number? What percentage do you assign yourself and the other person you are in relationship with for the quality of your relationships?

Being 100% responsible is the only place of personal power. You might find yourself objecting to this idea. What about the other person? What if that person is "x"? What if the person doesn't change? What if the other person won't cooperate? What I invite you to notice is where you are shining the light. You have the attention on the other person, which then places you as a victim of that person and their actions.

Often, in my work, I ask people "What percentage of responsibility do you accept for the quality (health) of your relationships?" I hear responses such as 50 percent, 70 percent, and 95 percent. My follow-up question is: how do you draw the line? It's interesting to hear people's different strategies they use to draw the line. If a person answers the first question with 99.99 percent, they have robbed themselves of power. Inherent to human beings is a tendency to blame, and even if the other person is .01% responsible, you've given yourself a "free" ticket to blame. And you will! Again, I say being 100% responsible is the only place of personal power.

While accountable and responsible are synonyms, I have a slightly different definition I've bought into for myself. I share it with you as an invitation to take on for yourself, and/or create your own empowering definition.

Responsible: being cause in the matter; answerable.

"Accountability: taking action that's consistent with our desired outcomes."

(Samuel & Chiche, 2004, p.xviii)

Holding people accountable in business is overused. I have not worked with an organization who didn't consider accountability an issue. The invitation through Personal Mastery and, specifically, responsibility is the opportunity for people to account to themselves. I believe that holding people accountable is a myth. We cause responsibility/accountability by way of the conversations we have when others don't honour their word or behave congruently with their commitments and values. Fundamentally, people can only choose to be responsible / accountable. I consider opportunities like these to be extraordinary as they are opportunities for individuals to be present to their greatness—to experience how big and powerful we really are as human beings.

What can you now be responsible for that you've previously been unwilling to be responsible for, so that you can produce your desired results?

PRESENT

"Your business is not to 'get somewhere'—it is to be here."

~ Dan Millman, Way of the Peaceful Warrior (1980, 1994, 2000)

What would it be like if you lived in the present moment?

Susannah, my client, says, "I'm exhausted. My minutes turn into hours, hours into days, days into weeks, weeks into months and months into years. Is this really how life is supposed to be? I'm so afraid nothing is going to change; I can't and won't go on like this." I wait with all of my attention on her. She continues, "I am unhappy and resentful of how busy I am. I am missing my children's upbringing, I don't have time for my family; and my husband and I rarely have a real conversation."

"What else?" I say.

"If I'm not disappointed with myself, I'm filled with guilt and shame or deathly afraid it will always be this way."

"What moments are you free of all that you've just described?" I ask. Space—she is looking.

She remembers and says, "The birth of my children, my mother's death, the night of my tenth wedding anniversary, the public announcement of my role as vice-president…" I wait. She continues with a few more moments in time, finishing with "Sunday morning in my garden."

"Please tell me about it." I encourage her.

She says, "It's early, five-ish; the sun is warm, I have my coffee beside me, and my hands are in the dirt. I am at peace. I remember mom loving early mornings in the garden; and now I know why. Life is good, I am at rest, my family is safe, we are loved; and the flowers are beautiful."

"What is the common thread throughout those moments in time?" I ask.

She looks at me, "I was present—nothing else mattered. I was in that moment without thought and attention on anything else."

"Given that that is the nature of life and you have chosen to live a life of busyness, how can you generate being present in all of it, at any given moment?" I ask.

Susannah's being resentful of the busyness of life, of what she is doing, and what she has to do, robs her of the present moment. Imagine the impact on Susannah's quality of life—and of her experience of herself—if she took a different stance: "I'm doing the perfect thing at the right time, in the perfect way and the perfect place."

How often do you dislike what you are doing?

What's the impact of resisting what you are doing in the present moment; therefore, on your life?

As human beings we either live in guilt about the past or fear of the future, forgetting that life is NOW! It sounds like, "I should have, I could have, I wish I would have." Replay, Churn, Guilt, Self-Criticism—they all consume time and energy, robbing us of seeing the good, appreciating and being present. Fear of the future sounds like, "I'll be happy when… I'll feel good when… I'll be satisfied when…," only to have "when" never arrive, keeping fulfillment out in the future. This has us unfulfilled now in the present moment and placing fulfillment out there sometime in the future.

Where do you live for the majority of your time?

DELIBERATE

How intentional are you as you show up in life?

> *"Real freedom is the ability to pause between stimulus and response—and in that pause—choose!"*
>
> *~ Rollo May (n.d.)*

There is a legend about a conversation between a grandson and his grandfather, a Cherokee chief. The grandson tells his grandfather that while he wants to protect his tribe, traditions, and family, he is afraid the majority of the time. The chief, in his wisdom, tells his grandson that each human being has a white wolf and a dark wolf. The white wolf is the bigger, greater, courageous part of us, while the dark wolf is the small, insecure and fearful part of us. He continues to share that each human being determines which wolf they feed moment-by-moment.

This story reminds me that each of us has a say over who we are being in the face of dealing with any human being and any given circumstance. Yet we live at the effect of life, as though our lives are determined by others and by circumstances.

"Forces beyond your control can take away everything you possess except one thing, your freedom to choose how to respond to the situation. You cannot control what happens to you in life, but you can always control what you will feel and do about what happens to you." (Frankl, 2006, Foreword p.2)

In what areas do you live life on purpose, and, conversely, where are you not living life on purpose?

"The ability to subordinate an impulse to a value is the essence of the proactive person."

~ Stephen R. Covey, The 7 Habits of Highly Effective People (1989, 2004)

Don is talking on the phone with me. He is yelling, "You promised me you would call me; and I get an email from your assistant instead."

I say, "You are right Don, I promised you I would pick up the phone any time I deal with you, and I didn't. I hear you are angry and hurt. You feel that you're not important to me (have the experience of being unimportant to me). What else?"

He swears. He shouts, "I will never do business with you again."

I respond, "I get it Don—I let you down. I didn't honour my word with you, and as a result you will never do business with me again. I'm committed to hearing everything you have to say. What else do you need to say to be complete?"

He swears several times, and again screams, "I will never do business with you again!"

I am aware of my reactions without giving myself to them. I am purposeful and deliberate about who I am being with and for him. I am holding a space for communication to clean this up. I am courageously committed that he is fully expressed about what it was like for him to have me break my promise to him. Our conversation continues for 45 minutes. Eventually he is no longer swearing and his tone is softening. There is nothing left unsaid; I got his communication —all of it: his words, his emotions, his feelings, and his experience.

He says, "We're in breakdown and need your help. When can you facilitate a conversation for us?" We land on a date and goals for our work together.

It would have been so easy and so messy to let myself react and be at the effect of the upset I caused with this client. Many would say I'd be justified in reacting to him given his anger and language.

We say we value something, but we react to others and situations in a way that is incongruent with what we say matters most to us. Being deliberate enables us to pay attention to what makes the greatest difference for ourselves and others and to fulfill on what really matters to us. Very few of us harness our own power by mastering the little one (the dark wolf).

We tend to live from the outside in versus the inside out. What I mean is that we focus on the results we want, what we must do or not do to produce the results we're after in order to be content, successful, accomplished, or satisfied (whatever experience we want). This is living life from the outside in.

Again, the only actual say we have in life is about who we are "being" in the face of dealing with people and any circumstance. Personal Mastery is exercising the power in each of us to create our "way of being" aligned with our desired results. We then become reliable to show up in a way of "being" that is congruent with our word. Exercising this power is what it means to live life on purpose—with intention. Building our muscle to be congruent in thought, word, and action is living life from the inside out. Our actions align with who we are "being," thereby, producing the outcomes we are committed to.

Imagine you need to have a difficult conversation with someone. You can go into that conversation being critical, frustrated, impatient, and demanding, and you will find yourself doing and saying certain things and producing a certain outcome. You can go into that very same conversation being direct, curious, compassionate, and patient, and you will find yourself doing and saying completely different things and producing a different result.

You, I, and every other human being on the planet have a say over "who we show up as" at any given moment.

Who are you aspiring to become?

INTEGRITY

> *"Without being a man or woman of integrity you can forget about being a leader. And, being a person of integrity is a never-ending endeavor. Being a person of integrity is a mountain with no top—you have to learn to love the climb."*
>
> ~ *Werner Erhard (2008, 2014)*

"I was a very young woman when I found the book *How to Become Your Own Best Friend*. I remember the impact of the concept that the fastest way to build self-esteem and confidence is to honour the promises I make to myself." (Owen, 1971).

It's Friday, November 5, 1999, about 6:30 pm. Darkness steps over dusk; nightfall settles in. There is a bitter chill in the air, claiming the space with hardness. I am running in North Glenmore Park, and I'm bundled in layers to protect me from the iciness. I am alone. I am present to the sting of the sleet hitting my eyes and the top of my cheekbones. The earth is still; the experience is surreal. I am the only person on the path; I am alone. I am filled with a sense of accomplishment, victory, and deep satisfaction. I am honouring a promise to myself, to go running Friday, after work. Throughout the day, I turn down invitations as I listen to the conversation in my head presenting all the reasons not to go running. Reasons such as I deserve to go out with friends, I've earned the right to go home to warmth and comfort, the weather is getting worse, the fatigue of the week is ever growing, and many others. I have many reasons to be anywhere other than on the path, running. There I am, moving one foot in front of the other, breathing deeply, pushing my pace. My confidence and sense of well-being expand, and as I enjoy the swell in my heart, I feel the pinch of the sleet, I relish the peacefulness of the space, and I am happy, in every way, with who I am.

At a base level, integrity is simply honouring our word.

We create mud pies; that is, we create unworkability in our relationships, in our families, and in our organizations when we don't honour our word. Covey (1989) coined the phrase "emotional bank account" to explain that when we do what we say we are going to do and in the time we said, we create a deposit of trust. When we don't do what we say we are going to do, we become unreliable, and a withdrawal of trust occurs. Often the withdrawals are much bigger than the deposits.

We erode our self-esteem, confidence, and sense of well-being when we don't honour our word. We erode our reliability and trustworthiness with others when we don't honour our word. We tend to minimize or entirely step over the broken promises.

What are the promises, big and small, that you've made and not honoured?

Erhard offers the following thoughts on self-deception about being out-of-integrity:

> People are mostly unaware that they have not kept their word. All they see is the 'reason,' rationalization or excuse for not keeping their word. In fact, people systematically deceive (lie to) themselves about who they have been and what they have done. As Chris Argyris concludes: "Put simply, people consistently act inconsistently, unaware of the contradiction between their espoused theory and their theory-in-use, between the way they think they are acting and the way they really act." And if you think this is not you, you are fooling yourself about fooling yourself. Because people cannot see their out-of-integrity behaviour, it is impossible for them to see the cause of the un-workability in their lives and organizations—the direct result of their own attempts to violate the Law of Integrity." (Erhard, 2010, p. 5)

What will you discover by cleaning up the mud pies in your life?

COURAGE

"Courage is not the absence of fear, but rather the judgment that something else is more important than fear."

~ Ambrose Redmoon (n.d.)

What fears have you been giving yourself to that if you took action, you would discover your courage?

It is close to midnight on October 21, 1995, as I leave the lodge at Camp Horizon in Kananaskis country, southwest of Bragg Creek, Alberta. I have spent the day learning a number of native traditions and rituals to use through the night on my "Vision Quest." I have a duffle bag over my shoulder containing a flashlight, a thermos of tea, a water bottle, bear mitts, my journal, markers and pen, and a few other things I was asked to bring.

As I'm stumbling through the darkness to find my perfect spot in the woods, I'm thinking, This is not what I thought it was going to be! I'm crazy to spend the night alone outside in the mountains so I can have a vision for my life come to me. When I signed up, my picture of a Vision Quest was a group of us dancing and chanting around a huge fire all night. Wrong!

I find my perfect spot and immediately perform two rituals that are supposed to protect me from being eaten in the night by a bear or something. As I sit there in the cold with the first snowfall of the season upon us, I'm acutely aware of a growing fear, anxiety, and near panic. As it grows, I believe I won't make it through the night and think about heading back to the lodge. I stop myself, recognizing that I'm giving myself to the fears and near-panic. I think, I registered for a reason; and I'm going to trust and go through the workshop as it's designed. I don't know what I'll learn or discover. I do know I can be courageous. I rest in that decision; it takes something for me to draw on courage, as opposed to fear, to make my decisions.

Courage is discovered through action; courage is not found in thinking about doing something. We have far more courage than we give ourselves credit for. Take action to discover your own courage.

The acorn becomes an oak by means of automatic growth; no commitment is necessary. The kitten similarly becomes a cat on the basis of instinct. Nature and being are identical in creatures like them. But a man or woman becomes fully human only by his or her choices and his or her commitment to them. People attain worth and dignity by the multitude of decisions they make from day by day. These decisions require courage.

~ Rollo May (n.d.)

Where will you get out of your own way and take action to fulfill a dream or goal that really matters to you?

AUTHENTIC

"What you get in your life is not a result of what you want; it is a result of who you are."

~ Marlon Smith (n.d.)

The greatest thing about being authentic is that the "real you" shows up. It is the "real" you and the "real me" that is attractive and engaging to others. We are far more attractive and engaging with others and in our own lives when we live authentically. It's a gift to the world and to ourselves when we give ourselves the freedom to be authentic. In doing so, we grant permission to others to be authentically their selves.

Michael says, "Hello."

"Hi Michael, it's Trudy, do you have a moment to talk?" As he says, "Yes," I think about how it's been six years since I have spoken to him. I say, "You said something to me when we broke up that I keep replaying in my mind, and now I understand why." I pause—silence. I continue, "I remember you saying you are not strong enough to be in a relationship with me. I never understood that comment and that's probably why I've never forgotten those words. I could not see what you were talking about until this morning. I see that you were never going to win with me. I now see that I cut you off at the knees every time we had a disagreement. I now see how hard I was on you. I was downright ugly and unkind. I apologize for being unloving. I am sorry for how I treated you."

Michael says, "Trudy, it wasn't all you. I had a big part in how things went down."

I say, "Thank you Michael. It's kind of you to say, and I own this. I did fall in love with you and while I did love you, I actually see I was being unloving. In our relationship, I actually was critical and demanding."

Michael expresses appreciation for my vulnerable and authentic conversation. We say good-bye with an experience of connection, completion, and freedom. We both know ourselves to be bigger in this moment.

What do you appreciate the most about yourself?

We all have a "false self" and a "real self." The false self is what we made up from the defining moments and decisions about ourselves and our life. The false self is limited, constrained, and we are trapped in a disempowering context; story. The false self is inauthentic.

> *"There's something liberating about not pretending.*
> *Dare to embarrass yourself. Risk."*
>
> ~ Drew Barrymore (n.d.)

What are you pretending not to know about yourself?

Taking a Walk on the Inside to meet ourselves is how we discover and be present with our "real self." We discover a new kind of experience of ourselves, others, and life when we get out of our own way and let ourselves be real. There is freedom, happiness, and connection when we are real. When we live authentically, we create power from being aligned and congruent with our true nature. Being authentic opens the door to seeing and appreciating humanity, the magic, and mystery of it all.

4. Why?

FULFILLMENT — AN EXTRAORDINARY LIFE

"The mass of men lead lives of quiet desperation. What is called resignation is confirmed desperation."

~ Henry David Thoreau (n.d.)

What is your fundamental experience of life?

It's March 2016, and I'm in Calgary with my mom and sister, Diane, visiting Aunt Areta.

Aunt Areta says, "When I came home after receiving the news I have cancer, I got on my knees in my bedroom and thanked God. I am so grateful it's me and not one of my children, grandchildren, or some young person who has their whole life ahead of them. I am 83 years old, I have lived a good life. Thank God it's me and not someone else."

It's now the end of April. This time I'm with my mom, visiting Aunt Areta. I am struck by her beauty as I wonder about the glow of love and light about her. We are talking about heartfelt gratitude and how it perhaps is supporting her body to deal with the treatment.

She says, "I remember years ago when I started the practice of gratitude each night just before I closed my eyes. The first time I did it, I struggled to find more than one thing to be grateful about. I stayed with the practice and soon enough, within weeks, I was falling asleep before I could finish thanking God for all the good in my life."

I am deeply moved and appreciate your faith and the congruence with which you live your life. Thank you, Aunt Areta, for sharing so generously.

One lives an extraordinary life by creating it now—exactly as life is and isn't. One is fulfilled by being fulfilled now—exactly as life is and as isn't.

What would you be, do, and have if you deliberately exercised your power to create?

You might be wondering "how?"

The answer is by thinking it is and looking for the extraordinary in all of it—the good, the bad, the ugly; by speaking about life as extraordinary, simply because you choose to live—and are committed to living—an extraordinary life. Take action to be big, to live in and from your personal power so that your experience of life is extraordinary.

> *"What we see depends mainly on what we look for."*
>
> ~ John Lubbock (n.d.)

What could you give up to let yourself see you are living an extraordinary life—now?

ACCEPTANCE AND FORGIVENESS

> *"Forgiveness means giving up all hope for a better past."*
>
> ~ Lily Tomlin (cited by E. Goldstein, 2010, 2011)

It's Easter weekend and I'm driving with my boyfriend to Whitecourt, so he can meet my family. We're having a great conversation as we get close to Red Deer, when he says, "I have to tell you something." I wait. He continues, "When I met you and started dating you, I was in relationship with someone else. I apologize I've withheld this from you."

WOW! I pull over to the side of the road, grab my phone, and dial Karen. When she answers, I say, "I need coaching. Do you have time?" She does. I am angry and hurt. I say, "Franco started our relationship on a lie; and he's been lying to me for three months." I vent, yell, scream, and cry until it's all out of me.

Karen says, "Trudy you can take the position that he lied to you, or you can stand in he's telling you the truth right now. Choose!"

The words hit me like a hammer. I say, "Thank you, I am choosing that he's telling me the truth." We say good-bye and I get in the car.

Franco looks terrified, I'm sure he's holding his breath. I turn to him saying, "I give up forever holding it against you that you lied to me and that lie hurt me." As I am making this promise to him, I think, I don't know if I can honour it, and in the next moment I wonder who I will become by doing so.

I honoured my promise. I never let my mind entertain the thought that he lied to me from that moment forward. It was a really cool and empowering experience of myself.

What is your context, both known and not known, of forgiveness?

My friend and colleague Kevin gave me this definition of forgiveness:

Give up forever holding it against someone that they did or didn't do "x" and therefore hurt you.

Giving up forever holding it against yourself that you did or didn't do "x" and therefore hurt someone, including yourself.

What will you forgive yourself for—right now?

Forgiveness is a gift you give yourself. Forgiveness is for you and you alone. Forgiving someone is an act of greatness that leaves us with the experience of grace.

Samuel and Chiche say this about the gift of forgiveness: "Once you have recognized the reality of what you are dealing with and owned the part you have played to get there, forgiveness is your way: Not an excuse to do something that didn't work again, but an opportunity to wipe the slate clean and give it another shot." (Samuel & Chiche, 2004, p. 55)

"People are illogical, unreasonable and self-centered. Love them anyway!"
~ Dr. Kent M. Keith (1968, 2001)

With whom and what conversation will you have such that you intend to complete with forgiveness?

FREEDOM AND CHOICE

"It's all invented anyway, so we might as well invent a story or a framework of meaning that enhances our quality of life and the life of those around us."

~ Benjamin Zander, The Art of Possibility (2002)

What does freedom mean to you?

What is your experience of choice in your life?

Executive vice-president Samuel and I are having our third coaching conversation. He says, "I'm at a great stage in my life and at a pivotal point in my career. I could become president and yet I'm doing things that actually risk my success, my personal relationships, and my well-being. I don't know who I am right now. I don't know why I'm doing what I'm doing—they are not good choices. It's dangerous for me, my career, and my family."

You and I have both the freedom and the power of choice to think and act independently of circumstances, conditions, and the assertions from others. You and I have both the freedom and the power of choice to think and act independently of our past.

To what degree do you exercise freedom and choice?

It takes tremendous courage to live a life of authentic freedom and choice. Living a life of authentic freedom and choice requires ongoing expansion in personal mastery and heightened attention, founded on commitment, vision, and discipline.

Living a life of authentic freedom and choice confronts what is inherent for human beings and the automaticity of being human. In other words, living a life of authentic freedom and choice threatens what is fundamental to what it means to be human. Living a life of authentic freedom and choice opposes the essential nature of human beings, the ways in which the brain is wired.

When I say "authentic freedom and choice," I'm describing an internal experience. It is the experience of being free on the inside to create yourself—aligned with your word, aspirations and heart's desire. It is powerfully choosing to be your "best" self, regardless of whether you have the experience of life as going your way, or the experience of life going against you. Living a life of authentic freedom and choice is a journey with the "unknown and unseen." This kind of life is a created life—now! And Now! And Now! Living a life of authentic freedom and choice demands our greatness to shine, demands that we complete our past and be responsible for how our life is and isn't. It's a life of dancing with, and tapping into, potential and possibility. Living a life of authentic freedom and choice requires us to wake up, to uncover and discover the "unknown already existing."

It's fall 2015. I'm approaching the end of my ninth year in business. I am anxious about cash flow given that my revenues are down. I feel exhausted, uninspired, and confused about what I really want to do. As I'm dealing with all of that, I'm invited to consider joining another firm that doesn't have the communication expertise in-house. They're expanding and growing at a fast pace, hitting the ceiling on capacity with existing resources. I have the experience of being the lone wolf in that I'm not collaborating the way I would like to. One of my first thoughts is what's wrong with me that I'm not growing and flourishing like them? I tell the founder I will consider it. On the way home, I talk on the phone with Henry and Judith, sharing where I am at and what I'm dealing with.

That evening, I Take a Walk on the Inside.

I walk through the major events as a business owner since the beginning, the good, the bad, and the ugly starting in year one. I explore what my internal conversations are about all that's happened and not happened. I go through the process of completion, creating peace and appreciation for all that I've been through. As I get closer to the present day, I am lit up. I am filled with appreciation for myself, recognizing the risks I've taken. I see I've lost some, I've won some, and it's all beautiful. I am grateful as I appreciate the people who supported me in my dream. I am free to create any kind of future; go with the new firm, play another ten years as president of Simply More Inc. I am authentically free to choose any path, to choose anything I want for myself and my life. I am empowered and excited as I create the possibilities and the strategy for the next ten years.

What action(s) could you take right now to expand your freedom and ability to choose?

VICTORY OVER THE PAST

> *"When I let go of what I am, I become what I might be."*
>
> *~ Lao Tzu (n.d.)*

Who would you be if your past didn't define you?

Victory over our past is a moment-by-moment phenomenon. It doesn't mean we don't have breakdowns and upset. That's not life. It's the victories in the moments when we "hit the ball out of the park" in the face of a big challenge. A victory is also dealing with and getting through breakdowns faster, with less wasted time and energy.

Fred is four years old when he and his sister are sent to live with their grandmother. Fred is a bed-wetter. Every day he gets a spanking from his grandmother for wetting the bed. One day as grandma is spanking him, Fred decides his mom doesn't love him. If she loved him, she would not have sent him away. It must mean he is not lovable.

When Fred is in his mid-forties, he overhears someone talk about his mother. In that moment, Fred comes face-to-face with the decision he made as a four-year-old and the impact on him, his mother and his family with so much time wasted.

He calls his mom that night and says, "I just discovered you love me." Fred shares with his mom what he made up when he was four years old. She starts to cry. She says, "Of all the things I've done in my life, my biggest regret is sending you and your sister to Vancouver."

Fred tells me, "I used to hate to talk with my mom; she bored me. After that call, I loved hearing her talk about her day. I enjoyed listening to her stories about bowling, her garden, and her life. I called her often to talk." I notice how lit up he is as he shares his transformation in his relationship with his mom.

He continues, *"A couple of years ago, she died of cancer. There was nothing left unsaid between us. There was only love—genuine, authentic love."*

Fred has a past. Fred discovered his "unknown, already existing" to free himself of his past. Fred is free. Fred has several victories over the past: not just with his mom—with every woman in his life.

I have a past. I am not my past. You have a past. You are not your past.

What is it that you do and who are you in the moments when you dislike yourself the most?

Covey introduced the concept of a "public and private" victory in his work *The Seven Habits of Highly Effective People* (1989). The private victories are the ones that really enable us to discover how big—how great—how magnificent each of us can be. It's those moments of victory where we are pure potential fulfilled. It becomes the fuel for playing a bigger game of Personal Mastery.

What would it be like to create a victory over that part of you and your past, moment-by-moment?

FULFILLMENT NOW

"True success, true happiness lies in freedom and fulfillment."

~ *Dada Vaswani (n.d.)*

What would it be like to let the moments of fulfillment in your life be enough?

I, like most human beings, have been in the trap of seeking something outside myself to be fulfilled. I, like you, have pursued success, happiness and fulfillment with the belief that it's something outside of myself that is going to fill me up. I am present to how much time and energy is wasted wanting to be fulfilled.

"I want my work to be meaningful. I want to know I am making a difference, and I want my work to matter. I want to be fulfilled." Katerina says.

93

"What would give you the experience of being fulfilled?" I ask. She is silent and we remain in the pause for a few minutes. I probe, "How do you measure whether your work is meaningful, and what makes it matter?" More silence.

"I don't know," she replies. We sit together, each in our own thoughts and hearts, wondering. "I don't think I know the experience of being fulfilled," she adds.

I invite her to create it. "Describe what you would have, who you would be, and what you would be doing if your work was meaningful and mattered, and you were fulfilled."

She struggles, again saying "I don't know."

Life is neutral!

We as human beings put meaning to our lives. We rarely give meaning that empowers us. We rarely frame our perceptions and interpretations to light us up and win. We habitually jump to conclusions and assumptions about others that show them in a negative light rather than focusing on a positive intention.

Robbie, Alicia, and I are on a Skype call. He says, "I've really been impacted by my holiday in Thailand."

I ask, "How so?"

He says, "They are so happy with so little. I'm humbled by it."

Every person on the planet—you and I—can choose to be fulfilled right now exactly as our life and as it isn't. There isn't anything from the outside that can authentically fulfill us. You can give up any experience of life you are having right now and generate yourself as fulfilled. Be fulfilled now and let yourself live an extraordinary life. You can. You deserve it. You are worthy of an extraordinary life.

What price are you and those closest to you paying as you let yourself live unfulfilled?

5. Conclusion

"I wish I could show you when you are lonely or in the darkness, the astonishing light of your own being."

~Hāfez (n.d.)

This book is about sharing and causing discoveries by "Taking a Walk on the Inside." It's an invitation for adventure matched with curiosity. This book invites you into an inquiry to uncover and discover that which is known, and not known. It is written to speak to your appetite for something more, whatever that more is for you that you want. It's a book that doesn't have any answers; and it is not about fixing you. You are perfect, whole, and complete.

My intention for you is to discover what it is to be human, from perspectives we all deal with. Each of us has been impacted by someone's need to be right. We've all stood in the position of being right; sometimes at all costs. All of us have been on the receiving end of being blamed, and all of us have blamed others and/or circumstances, letting ourselves be powerless in the face of circumstances. As human beings, we hang on to hurt, anger, frustration, and worries, and we end up resenting others; in many instances, ourselves and the very experiences we've lived. It's a book designed to presence and uncover the reactions and resistance we live out—versions of fighting life, being in our own way—and confronting the impact of all of that.

It's a book showcasing the automaticity of being human, revealing patterns, triggers; and the story in the background—including the "is" and the "am." The story is deeply embedded; it is not remembered as decisions made at an early age in life, thereby being lived as "true." My aspiration, through the questions I've asked, is to give you access to something new from seeing and remembering the story you made up.

This book is about possibilities, causing you to think differently about who you are and what's possible for you and your life. It's a book about leadership—self-directed leadership founded on Personal Mastery.

Personal Mastery is not a place to arrive at or somewhere to get to. Personal Mastery is a moment-by-moment created state that enables you and I to be "Masters" of ourselves in the face of any circumstance, including the times when the past, our triggers and actions, are driving our bus. From my journey, I've assembled seven elements for access to living life from, and in, personal power. I'm not talking about power over another or a situation; I'm talking about a command over oneself.

Why? For fulfillment, which I believe is a personal definition for each human being; for discovering and creating the experience of being extraordinary, for yourself and your life, as you Take a Walk on the Inside.

This book includes big ideas, not necessarily new ideas, about the definition and the power of both acceptance and forgiveness. This book asks you to discover and create anew what it is to be "free" and to live a life from a place of choice, leaving you victorious over yourself and/or your past.

That's what this book is about.

TWO QUESTIONS

When do I "Take a Walk on the Inside?"

Now…and Now….and Now!

Where do I start?

Wherever you are!

FOR YOU

You are amazing. I acknowledge you for your courage to "Take a Walk on the Inside."

FOR ME

I started, and didn't finish, writing this book on two other occasions over the last five years. As I prepare again and differently to write this book,

Tim passionately suggests on numerous occasions that I read *Big Magic* (2015) by Elizabeth Gilbert.

It's Boxing Day and we are driving to Castlegar, listening to the audio version of *Big Magic*, which is narrated by Elizabeth Gilbert. Thank you, Elizabeth. I know I will start and finish the book as I am inspired by three insights I get from her work.

The first is, "Your work is important and your work isn't important." Cool, it's not significant, so get out of my own way.

The second, "Just go make something."

The third, and the biggest, take-away I got from her work is the idea of answering the question, "Who am I writing this book for?"

It pops. I'm writing the book for me; just to discover who I will become through the experience of writing a book.

This is my created context for the book. As with life itself, it's been a roller coaster ride. An extraordinary experience of myself, creative flow, and piercing clarity; moments in the mirror confronting my crazy ideas I could actually do this, and moments in the mirror reminding myself I invented this experience and I have my word in the matter.

This bold undertaking is for me... And for you...

> *"What you do for your Self, you do for another. What you do for another, you do for your Self."*
>
> ~ Neale Donald Walsch, *Conversations with God (1996)*

Bibliography

Anderson, G. (n.d.) "Greg Anderson Quotes," quoteland.com (2001). http://www. quoteland.com/author/Greg-Anderson-Quotes/2683/ (Retrieved April 30, 2016).

Barrymore, D. (n.d.)."Drew Barrymore Quotes," brainyquote.com (2016). http://www.brainyquote.com/quotes/quotes/d/drewbarrym129647.html (Retrieved April 30, 2016).

Beckwith, M.B. (n.d.) "Michael Beckwith Quotes," addicted2success.com (2016). http://addicted2success.com/quotes/32-inspirational-michael-bernard-beckwith-quotes/ (Retrieved April 30, 2016).

Brown, B. (2010). *The Gifts of Imperfection: Let Go of Who You Think You're Supposed to Be and Embrace Who You Are.* Central City, MN: Hazelden.

Carnegie, D. (1981). *How to Win Friends and Influence People.* New York, NY: Simon & Schuster, Inc.

Casey, S. (2012). *Belief Repatterning: The Amazing Technique for "Flipping the Switch" to Positive Thoughts.* Bloomington, IN: Hay House Insights.

Covey, S.R. (1989, 2004). *The 7 Habits of Highly Effective People: Powerful Lessons in Personal Change.* New York, NY: Simon & Schuster.

da Vinci, L. (n.d.)."Leonardo da Vinci Quotes," goodreads.com (2016). www.good reads.com/quotes/8684-one-can-have-no-smaller-or-greater-mastery-than-mastery (Retrieved April 30, 2016).

de Montaigne, M. (1987, 1991, 2003). *The Complete Essays.* (M.A. Screech, Trans. & Ed.). London, UK: Penguin Books.

Dispenza, D. J. (2012). *Breaking the Habit of Being Yourself: How to Lose Your Mind and Create a New One.* New York, NY: Hay House, Inc.

Einstein, A. (n.d.)."Albert Einstein Quotes," brainyquote.com (2016). http://www. brainyquote.com/quotes/quotes/a/alberteins145949.html (Retrieved April 30, 2016).

Epictectus (n.d.) "Epictectus Quotes," brainyquote.com (2016). http://www.brainy quote.com/quotes/quotes/e/epictetus149126.html (Retrieved April 30, 2016).

Erhard, W.H., Jensen, M.C., Zaffron, S., & Echeverria, J.L. (August 2008, Revised July 2014). "Introductory Reading for Being A Leader and the Effective Exercise of Leadership: An Ontological/Phenonmenological Model." *Harvard Business School Negotiation, Organizations and Markets Research Papers*, 33: 1-105.

Erhard, W.H., Jensen, M. C., & Zaffron, S. (First Draft January 2010, Revised 2014, March 25). "Integrity: A Positive Model That Incorporates The Normative Phenomena Of Morality, Ethics, And Legality Abridged." *Harvard Business School Working Paper No. 10-061*, February 2010.

Feldman, C. (2003). *Silence: How to Find Inner Peace in a Busy World*. Berkeley, CA: Rodmell Press.

Ford, H. (n.d.), "Henry Ford Quotes," brainyquote.com (2016). http://www.brainy quote.com/quotes/quotes/h/henryford122851.html (April 30, 2016).

Foster, C. (1993). *The Family Patterns Workbook: Breaking Free from Your Past & Creating A Life of Your Own*. New York, NY: Jeremy P. Tarcher/Pedigree Books.

Frankl, V. E. (2006). *Man's Search For Meaning*. Boston, MA: Beacon Press.

Galilei, G. (n.d.) "Galileo Galilei Quotes," quotationspage.com (2015). http://www.quotationspage.com/quotes/Galileo_Galilei/ (Retrieved April 30, 2016).

Gide, A. (n.d.) "André Gide Quotes," brainyquote.com (2016). http://www.brainy quote.com/quotes/quotes/a/andregide120088.html. (Retrieved April 30, 2016).

Goleman, D. (2005) *Emotional Intelligence. Why It Matters More than IQ* (10th Anniversary Edition). New York, NY: Bantam Dell.

Hāfez (n.d.). "Quote by Hāfez," quotery.com. http://www.quotery.com/quotes/i-wish -i-could-show-you-when-you-are-lonely/ (Retrieved April 30, 2016).

Hicks, A. (n.d.) "Abraham Hicks Quotes," google.ca (n.d.) https://www.google.ca search?q=The+story+I+live+is+created+by+the+story+I+tell+myself.+~+ Abraham+Hicks&biw=1224 &bih= 707&source=lnms&tbm=isch&sa=X&ved =0ahUKEwjKzumGj97NAhXm24MKHWYk BckQ_ AUIBygC#imgrc=0pqlp 1XHHD8SxM%3A (Retrieved April 30, 2016).

Hicks, E. & J. Hicks (The Teachings of Abraham). (2007). *The Astonishing Power of Emotions: Let Your Feelings Be Your Guide*. Carlsbad, CA: Hay House.

Hurson, T. (2008). *Think Better (your company's future depends on it...and so does yours)*. New York, NY: McGraw-Hill.

Jung, C.G. (n.d.). "C.G. Jung Quotes" goodreads.com (2016). http://www.goodreads.com/quotes/485998-what-you-resist-persists (Retrieved April 30, 2016).

Kahle, D. (2008). *Question Your Way to Sales Success*. Pompton Plains, NJ: Career Press.

Katie, Byron & S. Mitchell. (2002). *Loving What Is: Four Questions That Can Change Your Life*. New York, NY: Harmony Books.

Keith, Dr. K.M. (1968, 2001). *Anyway. The Paradoxical Commandments*. http://www.paradoxicalcommandments.com/ (Retrieved April 30, 2016).

Kennedy, J.F. (n.d.). "John F. Kennedy Quotes," brainyquote.com (2016). http://www.brainyquote.com/quotes/quotes/j/johnfkenn130752.html (Retrieved April 30, 2016).

Kierkegaard, S. (n.d.). "Søren Kierkegaard Quotes," brainyquote.com (2016). http://www.brainyquote.com/quotes/quotes/s/sorenkierk152222.html (Retrieved April 30, 2016).

King, M.L. Jr. (n.d.) "Yoga Gems Quotes," sattvayoga.ca. http://sattvayoga.ca/gems.html (Retrieved April 30, 2016).

Lao Tzu (n.d.). "Lao Tzu Quotes," brainyquote.com (2016). http://www.brainyquote.com/quotes/quotes/l/laotzu386562.html and http://www.brainyquote.com/quotes/quotes/l/laotzu379182.html (Retrieved April 30, 2016).

"leadership" *dictionary.com*.(2016). http://www.dictionary.com/browse/leadership. (Retrieved April 30, 2016).

Lawrence, T.E. (n.d.). "T.E. Lawrence Quotes," elise.com (n.d.). http://www.elise.com/q/quotes/lawrence.htm (Retrieved April 30, 2016).

Lee, B. (n.d.), "Bruce Lee Quotes," goodreads.com (2016). www.goodreads.com/quotes/48714-empty-your-cup-so-that-it-may-be-filled-become (Retrieved April 30, 2016).

Lencioni, P. (2002). *The Five Dysfunctions of a Team: A Leadership Fable*. San Francisco, CA: Jossey-Bass.

Lipton, B. & Bhaerman, S. (2009). *Spontaneous Evolution: Our Positive Future And A Way To Get There From Here.* Carlsbad, CA: Hay House.

Lubbock, J. (n.d.) "John Lubbock Quotes," brainyquote.com (2016). http://www.brainy quote.com/quotes/quotes/j/johnlubboc107112.html (Retrieved April 30, 2016).

Marshall, P (Director). (1992) *A League of Their Own* (Film). Los Angeles, CA: Columbia Studios.

Maurois, A. (n.d.). "André Maurois Quotes," IZQuotes.com (n.d.). http://izquotes.com/ quote/251476 (Retrieved April 30, 2016).

May, R. (n.d.). "Rollo May Quotes," azquotes.com. http://www.azquotes.com/quote/ 845546 (Retrieved April 30, 2016).

May, R. (n.d.). "Rollo May Quotes," gaiam.com (2016). http://blog.gaiam.com/quotes/ authors/rollo-may-0/31606 (Retrieved April 30, 2016).

Millman, D. (1980, 1984, 2000). *Way of the Peaceful Warrior: A Book That Changes Lives.* Tiburon, CA: H.J. Kramer Inc.

"objectify" *dictionary.com.* (2016). http://www.dictionary.com/browse/objectify. (Retrieved April 30, 2016).

Owen, M. N. (1971). *How To Be Your Own Best Friend.* New York, NY: The Random House Publishing Group.

Proust, M. (n.d.). "Proust Quotes," goodreads.com (2016). http://www.goodreads. com/quotes/33702-the-real-voyage-of-discovery-consists-not-in-seeking-new (Retrieved April 28, 2016).

Pythagoras (n.d.) "Pythagorus Quotes," goodreads.com (2016). http://www.good reads.com/quotes/111887-no-one-is-free-who-has-not-obtained-the-empire (Retrieved April 30, 2016).

Redmoon, A. (n.d.). "Ambrose Redmoon Quotes," thinkexist.com (2016). http:// thinkexist.com/quotes/ambrose_redmoon/ (Retrieved April 30, 2016).

"responsible" *dictionary.com* Unabridged. (2016). http://www.dictionary.com/browse/ responsible. (Retrieved May 23, 2016).

Rohr, R. (n.d.). "Richard Rohr Quotes," goodreads.com (2016). https://www.goodreads.com/work/quotes/550272-breathing-underwater-spirituality-and-the-12-steps (Retrieved April 30, 2016).

Rubin, M. (n.d.) "Marty Rubin Quotes," goodreads.com (2016). http://www.goodreads.com/quotes/493871-in-my-travels-i-found-no-answers-only-wonders (Retrieved April 30, 2016).

Ruiz, D.M. (1997). *The Four Agreements: A Practical Guide to Personal Freedom.* San Rafael, CA: Amber-Allen Publishing.

Samuel, M. & Chiche, S. (2004). *The Power of Personal Accountability: Achieve What Matters to You.* Katonah, NY: Xephor Press.

Scott, S. (2002, 2004). *Fierce Conversations. Achieving Success at Work & In Life, One Conversation at a Time.* New York, NY: The Berkley Publishing Group.

Senge, P. (1996, 2000). *The Fifth Discipline: The Art & Practice of the Learning Organization.* New York, NY: Doubleday.

Shaw, G.B. (n.d.) "George Bernard Shaw Quotes," brainyquote.com (2016). http://www.brainyquote.com/quotes/quotes/g/georgebern109542.html (Retrieved April 30, 2016).

Smith, M. (n.d.) "Authenticity," clarityesd.com (2016). http://www.clarityesd.com/authenticity.html (Retrieved April 30, 2016).

Socrates. (n.d.). "Socrates Quotes," brainyquote.com (2016). http://www.brainyquote.com/quotes/quotes/s/socrates101168.html (Retrieved April 28, 2016).

Socrates. (n.d.). "Socrates Quotes," goodreads.com (2016). http://www.goodreads.com/quotes/4097-wonder-is-the-beginning-of-wisdom (Retrieved April 28, 2016).

Socrates (n.d.) "I know that I know nothing," Wikipedia.org (n.d.) https://en.wikipedia.org/wiki/I_know_that_I_know_nothing (Retrieved April 30, 2016).

Thoreau, H.D. (n.d.). "Henry David Thoreau Quotes," brainyquote.com (2016). http://www.brainyquote.com/quotes/quotes/h/henrydavid106411.htm (Retrieved April 30, 2016).

Tomlin, L. (n.d.) cited by E. Goldstein in "The Blog: Forgiveness Means Giving Up All Hope For a Better Past," in huffingtonpost.com (June 23, 2010, updated

November 17, 2011). http://www.huffingtonpost.com/elisha-goldstein-phd/forgiveness-means-giving_b_620158.html (Retrieved April 30, 2016.)

Vaswani, D. (n.d.) "Dada Vaswani Quotes," brainyquote.com (2016). http://www.brainy quote.com/quotes/quotes/d/dadavaswan532442.html (Retrieved April 30, 2016).

Wallace, D.F. (n.d.) "David Foster Wallace Quotes," goodreads.com (2016). http://www.goodreads.com/quotes/968249-you-can-t-unring-a-bell (Retrieved April 30, 2016.)

Walsch, N.D. (1996). *Conversations with God: An Uncommon Dialogue, Vol 1.* New York, NY: G.P. Putnam's Sons.

"wonder" dictionary.com. (2016). http://www.dictionary.com/browse/wonder. (Retrieved April 28, 2016).

Yeats, W.B. (n.d.) "W.B. Yeats Quotes," goodreads.com (2016). http://www.goodreads.com/quotes/122468-the-world-is-full-of-magic-things-patiently-waiting-for (Retrieved April 30, 2016).

Yoda (n.d.) Yodaquotes.net. http://www.yodaquotes.net/ (Retrieved April 30, 2016).

Zander, R.S. & B. Zander, B. (2002). *The Art of Possibility: Transforming Professional and Personal Life.* New York, NY: Penguin Group.

Index

known/not known, 36–38, 45, 47–48, 89

About the Author

Trudy is a communication specialist who facilitates conversations to expand communication and leadership capacity, which resolves the toughest issues leaders face. Trudy is passionate about connecting people to their personal power. Trudy's leadership style calls greatness forward for the development of human beings.

Trudy Pelletier is founder of Simply More Inc., a FAMILY ENTERPRISE ADVISOR™ certificant, a certified executive coach and certified in Emotional Intelligence and Fierce Conversations®.

Main Website: www.simplymore.ca
Blog: www.simplymore.ca/blog
LinkedIn: www.linkedin.com/in/trudypelletier
Facebook: www.facebook.com/trudy.pelletier.9
         www.facebook.com/SimplyMoreInc
Twitter: www.twitter.com/trudypelletier
YouTube: www.youtube.com/channel/UCjT5taSQClr7yby8wm79fVQ